SEAN DELONAS

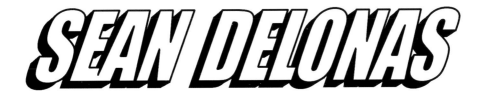

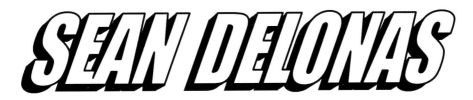

SEAN DELONAS

THE ONES THEY DIDN'T PRINT AND
SOME OF THE ONES THEY DID

201 Cartoons

SEAN DELONAS

Foreword by Dan Aquilante, former *New York Post* music critic

Skyhorse Publishing, Inc.

Skyhorse Publishing books may be purchased in bulk at special discounts for sales promotion, corporate gifts, fund-raising, or educational purposes. Special editions can also be created to specifications. For details, contact the Special Sales Department, Skyhorse Publishing, 307 West 36th Street, 11th Floor, New York, NY 10018 or info@skyhorsepublishing.com.

Skyhorse® and Skyhorse Publishing® are registered trademarks of Skyhorse Publishing, Inc.®, a Delaware corporation.

Visit our website at www.skyhorsepublishing.com.

10 9 8 7 6 5 4 3 2 1

Library of Congress Cataloging-in-Publication Data is available on file.

Cover design by Sean Delonas and Brian Peterson
Cover illustrations credit Sean Delonas
Cartoons by John Delonas reproduced on page 11 with permission by Nadia Delonas

Print ISBN: 978-1-63220-365-6
Ebook ISBN: 978-1-63220-839-2

Printed in China

CONTENTS

For my mother, father, and son

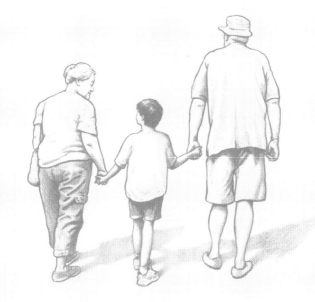

FOREWORD

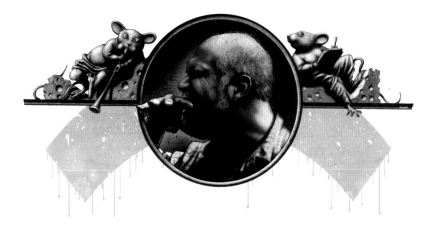

If he was a normal person—like you or me—it might be fair to tag Sean Delonas as a perversely evil misanthrope. A man poised to pounce on the missteps of icons and idiots with equal contempt.

But Delonas isn't an evil genius; he's just a 6'4", 250-pound man-child who happens to be a master draftsman. He can draw, paint, or sculpt anything, but usually that anything is a woebegone politico or a celebrity who's recently ruined his or her life with a very bad public choice.

According to Mark Twain, "Humor is tragedy plus time." Delonas once actually tested Twain's theory with a block cartoon of a Ford Theater usher asking Mary Todd Lincoln, "Other than that, how was the play?" Whether it was just an old joke that still has a little laughing gas in it or Abe's expression—X's for eyes and his tongue lolling from his mouth—but that panel is plain funny.

More often Delonas found himself in hot water with both his editors at the *Post* and his readership because his work rarely enjoyed the luxury of time in that classic comedy equation.

One of those all-too-soon laughs that incited a vicious public backlash was over a panel cartoon about the infamous lip-sync duo Milli Vanilli. In this sketch MV front man Rob Pilatus, who had just OD-ed in real life, is drawn flat on his back apparently asking for medical help. A befuddled cop can't understand the nature of the emergency because, as the cops says, "His lips are moving but nothing's coming out."

It's okay to smile—Delonas is a guilty pleasure.

How about when Michael Jackson was acquitted on charges of sexual misconduct with a minor? Delonas illustrated that breaking news with a cartoon of the King of Pop sitting at the dinner table with his closest pals including the bones of the elephant man, Bubbles the chimp, and an anaconda. MJ declares, "With the trial over things can get back to normal around here."

It was a very good cartoon, but the one Delonas really wanted to appear, but was rejected by *Post* editors as "too far over the edge," was MJ hugging a young boy in celebration of his acquittal. In this frame it appears the Gloved-one's "lost" mitten could be found in the waistband of the youngster's shorts. True, that cartoon was rejected, yet it made it into the paper anyway because mischievous Delonas drew it as a framed wall-painting in the background of the "back to normal" panel. And Sean Delirious thought nobody would notice.

Be you a president or a pastor you were never safe from Delonas's very sharp pencil. After Rev. Al Sharpton once compared his work with that of Martin Luther King Jr., Delonas was inspired to draw a rare two panel cartoon. One with Dr. King delivering his famous line, "I have a dream"; the second with the self-promoting Sharpton uttering, "I have a scheme."

President Bill Clinton's sexual appetites were often fodder for Delonas, who liked to draw Clinton in luv-print boxer shorts holding a power drill attached to a spinning fish. When asked, "What gives with the fish-drill?" Delonas would admit he didn't know, but he liked how the odd semi-sexual device would fire people's imaginations as to its use. That's one of Delonas's secrets: he makes us complicit in his madness.

And as for that monkey, all I can say is if Delonas intended it to be President Obama it would have had bigger ears.

To understand Delonas's fuck-'em-if-they-can't-take-a-joke attitude you have to loosen up and be ready to be offended.

His holiday cartoon of an elephant, a duck, a gorilla, and a giraffe all hitched to Santa's sleigh explains the man perfectly. After looking at the menagerie replacing Rudolf and the other reindeer, you have to agree with the elf telling Santa, "I think we're getting carried away with this political correctness." Amen.

Dan Aquilante, December 2014

INTRODUCTION

My father drew cartoons. My earliest memories are scribbling cartoons with him at the kitchen table. Some things about my father's life are known to me only through his cartoons—experiences of war, his youth (notice the cat drinking and smoking in the cartoon "Hugh of Drew (and Kinsey, the Cat)"), women, and so on. Luckily, my cartoons say nothing about me.

In 1990, my life changed after drawing a portrait of the late, great Bay Rigby (pictured right). Bay was the *New York Post*'s Page Six cartoonist and son of the famed *Daily News* cartoonist, Paul Rigby.

Bay wanted to go back to Australia and asked if I would fill in for him for three months at the *Post*. Managing editor Lou Colasuonno hired me. The first person I told was my father. For the rest of his life, my father called me at work with ideas and always would hand me several pages of drawings at every family get together.

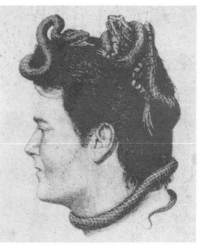

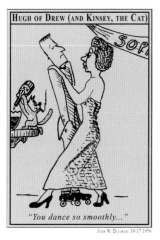

HUGH OF DREW (AND KINSEY, THE CAT)

"You dance so smoothly..."

John W. Delonas, 10/17/1956

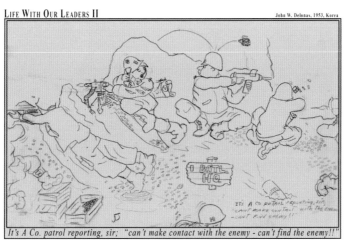

LIFE WITH OUR LEADERS II

John W. Delonas, 1953, Korea

It's A Co. patrol reporting, sir; "can't make contact with the enemy - can't find the enemy!!"

Almost twenty-three years, and nearly six thousand cartoons after taking a temporary three-month job, I accepted a buyout. My career with the *New York Post* ended on May 31, 2013. The National Review Online wrote, "Sean Delonas Has Left the *New York Post*. Page Six just won't be the same without him."

Scribbling with my father led to something bigger than I ever dreamed.
Thanks, Dad.

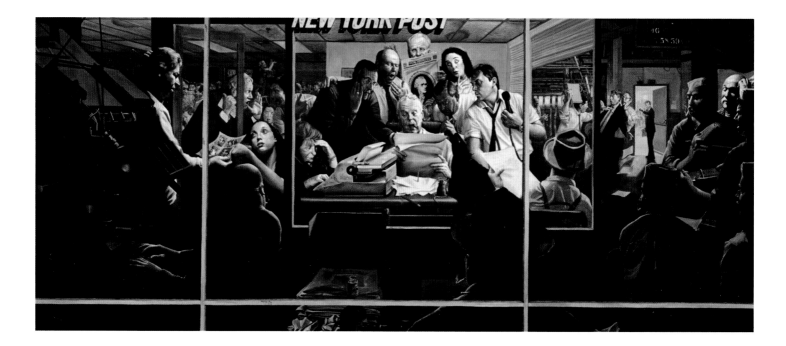

CELEBRITIES

AND DOES KIM'S AGENT, TAKE KANYE'S AGENT, 'TIL THE PUBLICITY STOPS DO THEY PART...
DELONAS

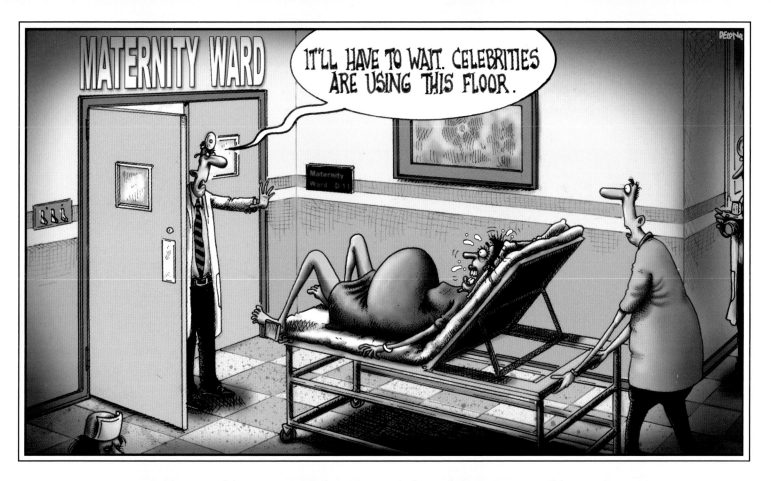

Beyonce's delivery occupies the entire sixth floor of NYC's Lenox Hill hospital.

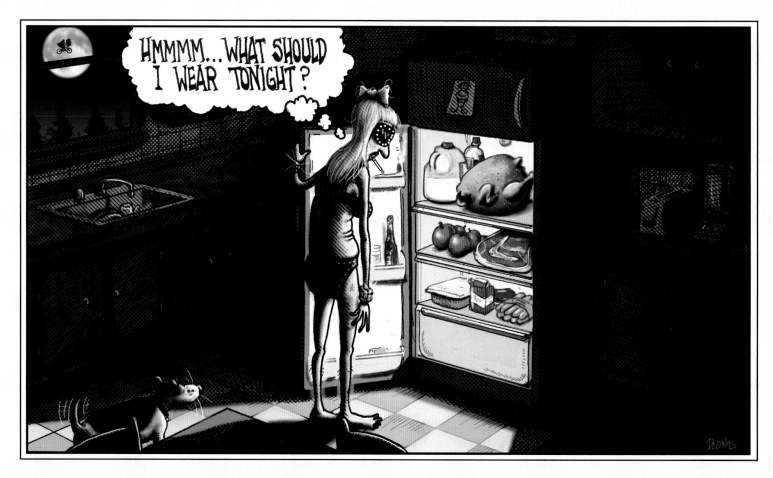

Lady Gaga wears a meat dress to the 2010 Video Music Awards.

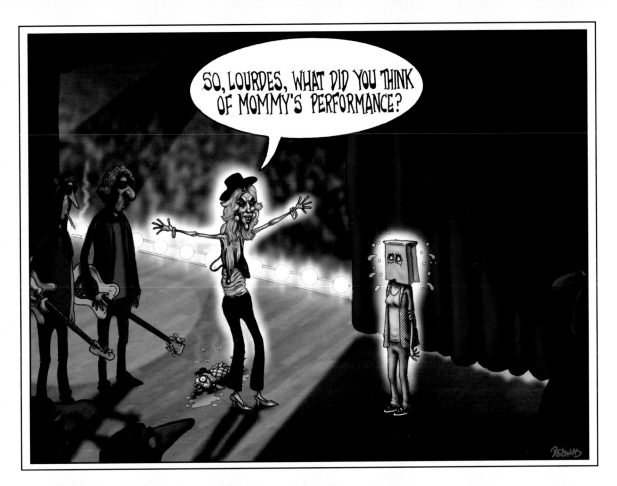

If most teens are embarrassed when their parents do nothing, what must Lordes think of her mother, Madonna, exposing her breast at a concert in Istanbul?

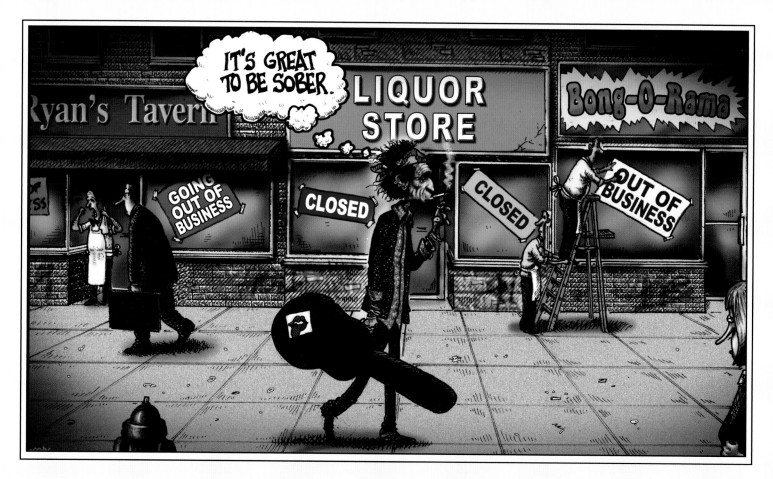

Keith Richards gives up booze and drugs.

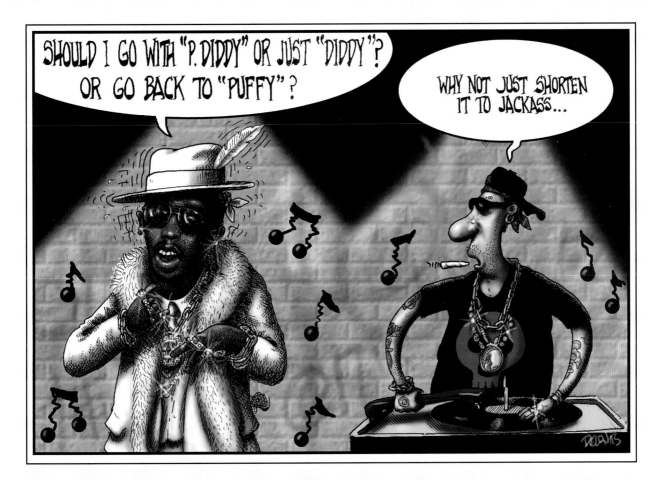

Sean Combs, a.k.a. Puffy, Puff Daddy, Diddy, P. Diddy, etc., announces that he's considering another name change.

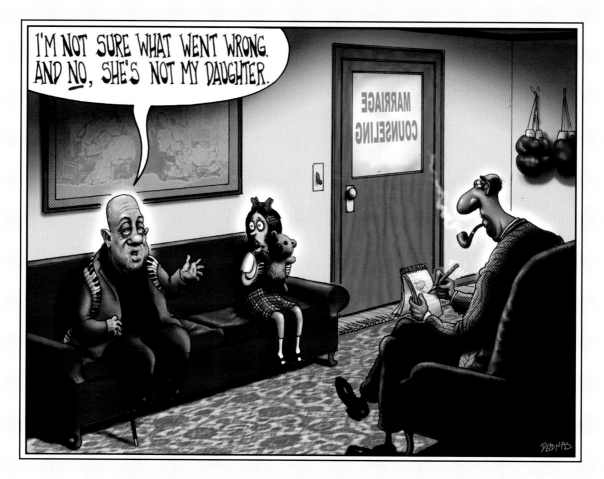

Billie Joel trying to figure out what went wrong with his marriage.

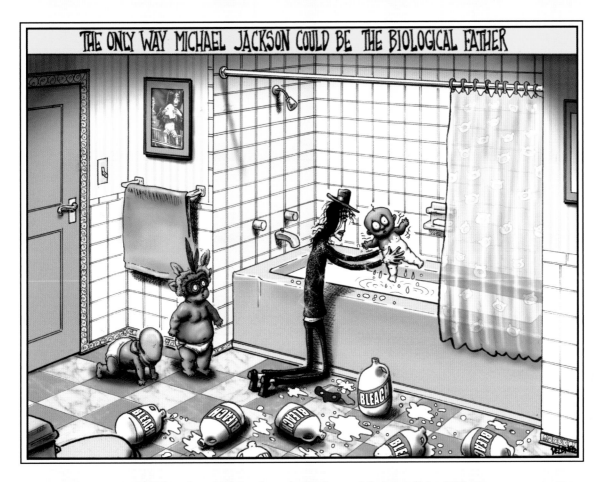

Michael Jackson insists he's the biological father of his children.

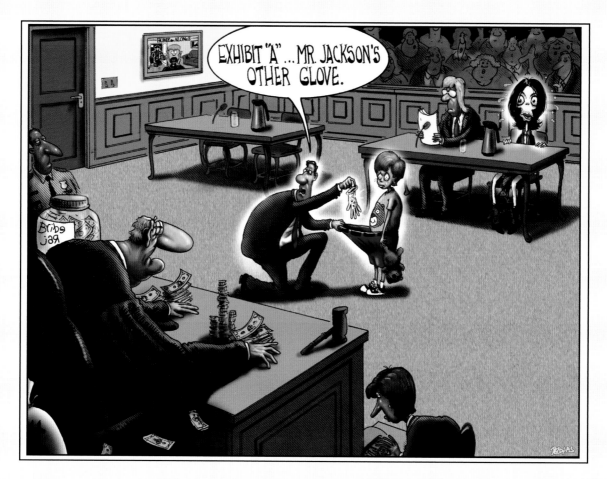

Michael Jackson on trial for sexual abuse of a minor.

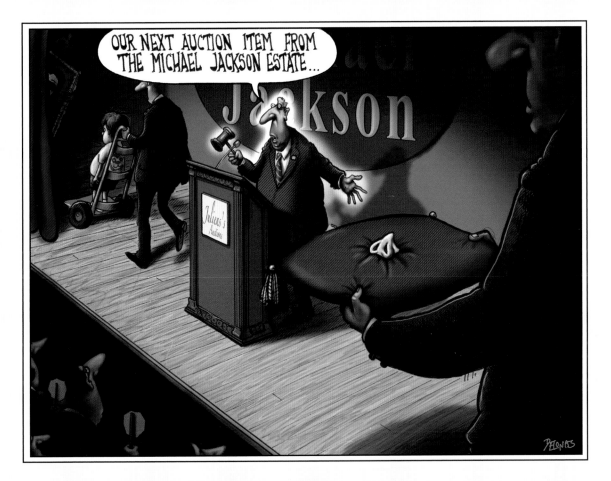

Michael Jackson's estate is up for auction.

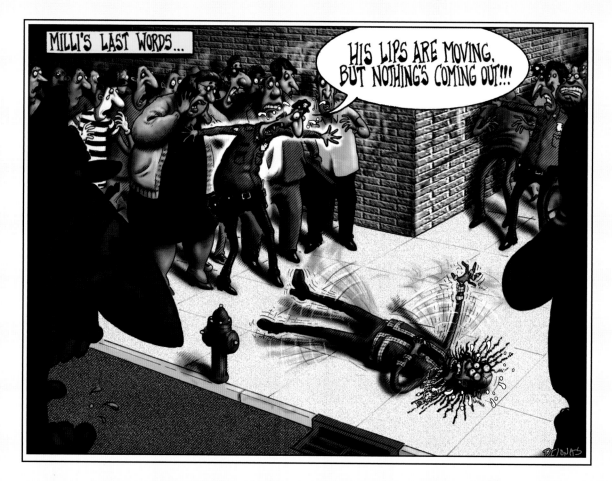

Death of Milli, from the lip-singinging sensation, Milli Vanilli

MAKE THAT A DOUBLE...I'M DRINKING FOR TWO NOW.

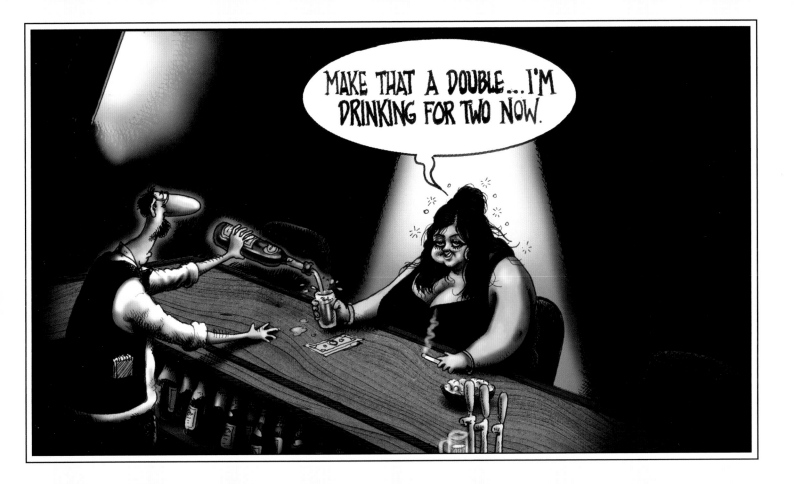

MATERNITY WARD
WHICH ONE IS OURS, SNOOKI?

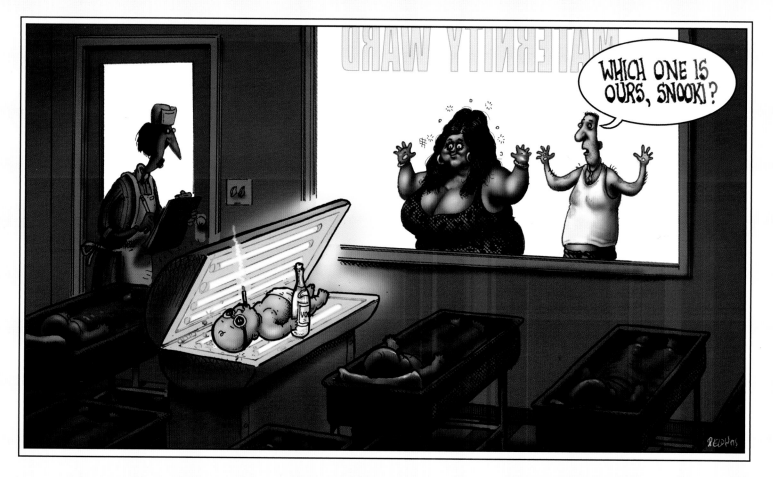

Snooki has a baby.

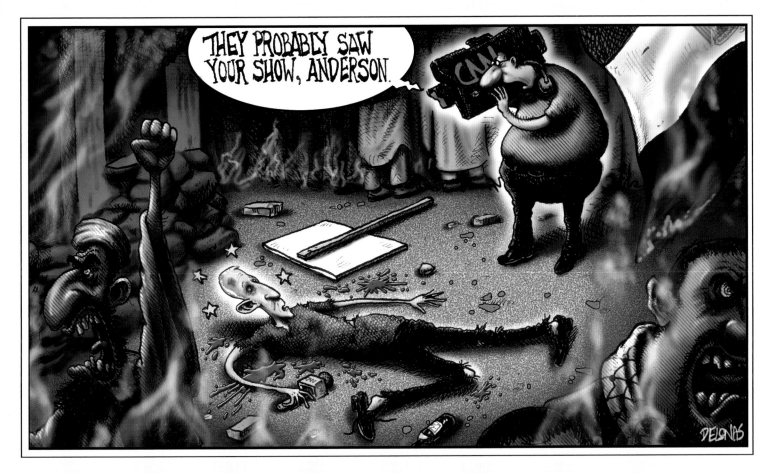

CNN's Anderson Cooper is beaten up during Egypt's Arab Spring.

HECTOR, FROM MY BEDROOM.
GO AHEAD CALLER.
TAKING YOUR CALLS
CNN
Cheating Spouses
LARRY
KING
LIVE
DELONAS

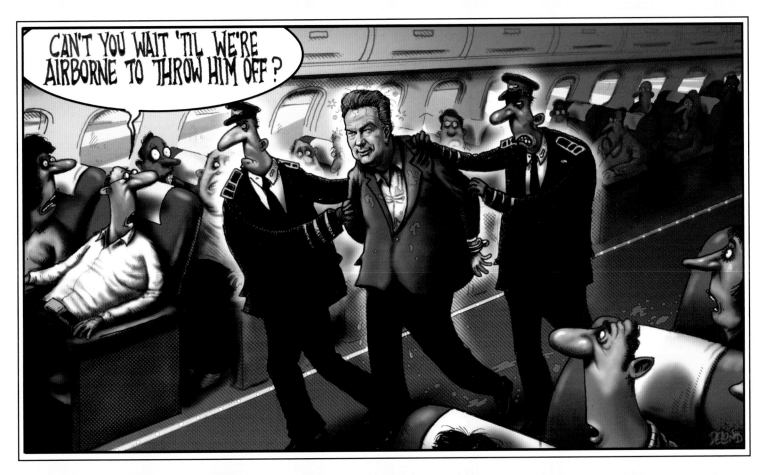

Alec Baldwin thrown off an AA flight at LAX for using his cell phone.

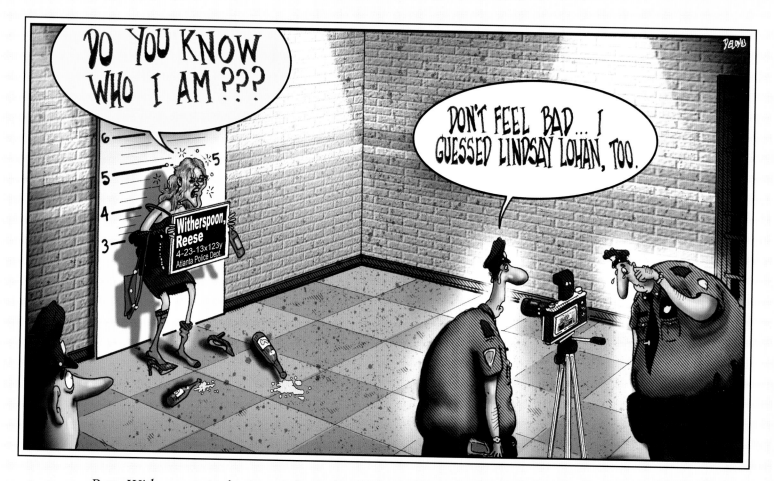

Reese Witherspoon is abusive to police, yelling, "Do you know who I am?" as her husband is arrested for a DUI. Reese is also arrested.

LET ME ASSURE YOU MY CLIENT, MS. LOHAN, IS NOT A THIEF.

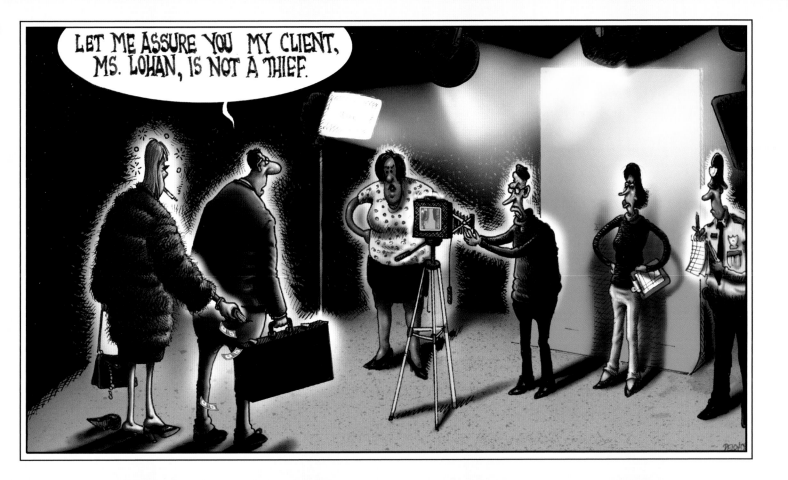

LINDSAY LOHAN GETS HER DRIVER'S LICENSE BACK
PARKING
EXIT
ENTRANCE
PIZZA
OPEN

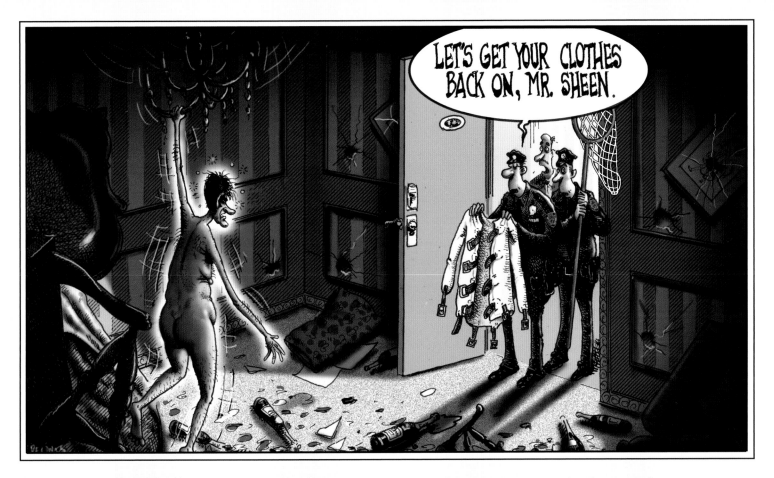

According to police, an intoxicated, naked Charlie Sheen tore up his suite at the Plaza Hotel.

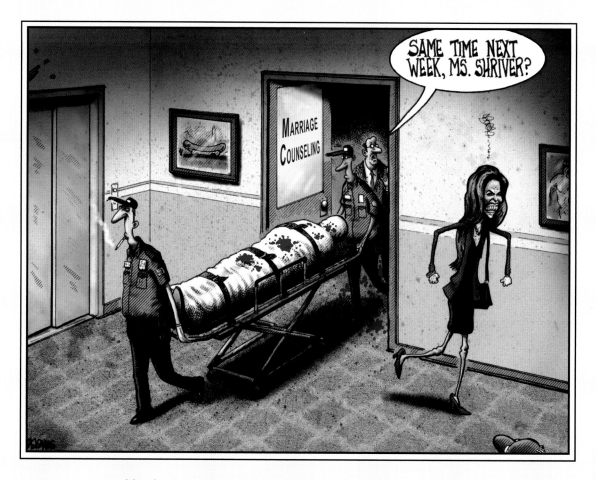

Arnold Schwarzenegger and Maria Shriver go to marriage counseling.

SHOULD'VE MADE THE HOLE DEEPER...
ANNA NICOLE SMITH
DELONAS

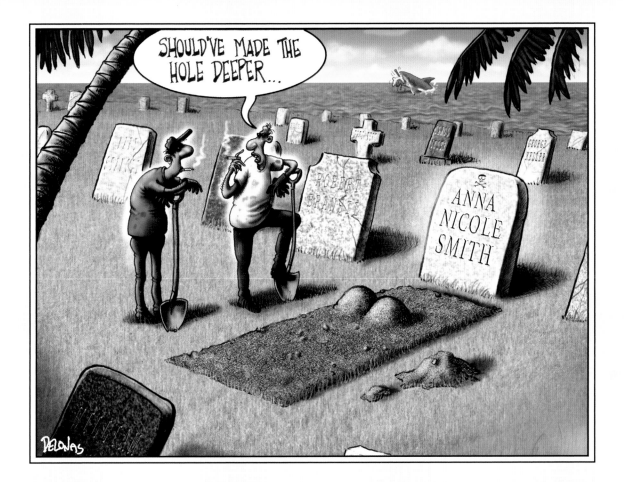

NO, NO, MS. HILTON, I MEANT INTO THE BREATHALYZER!!!
DELONAS

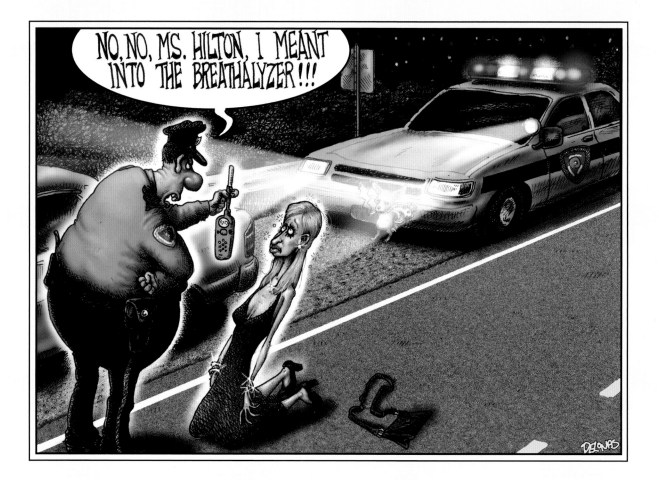

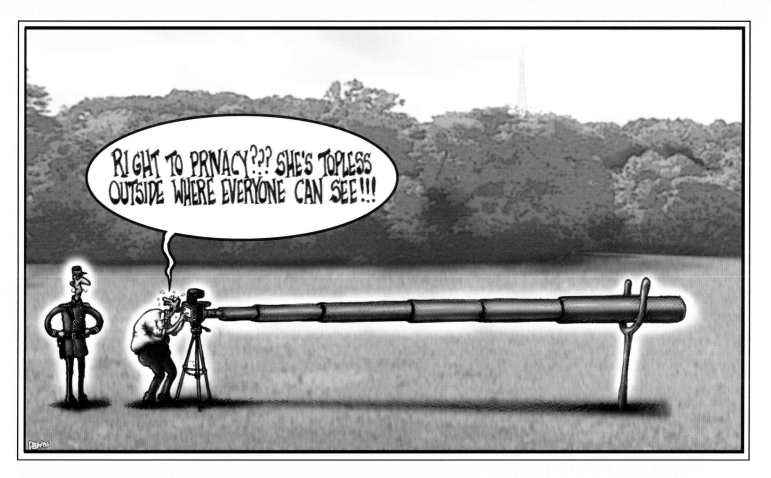

Kate Middleton photographed sunbathing topless from over a mile away. French magazine Closer published the photos.

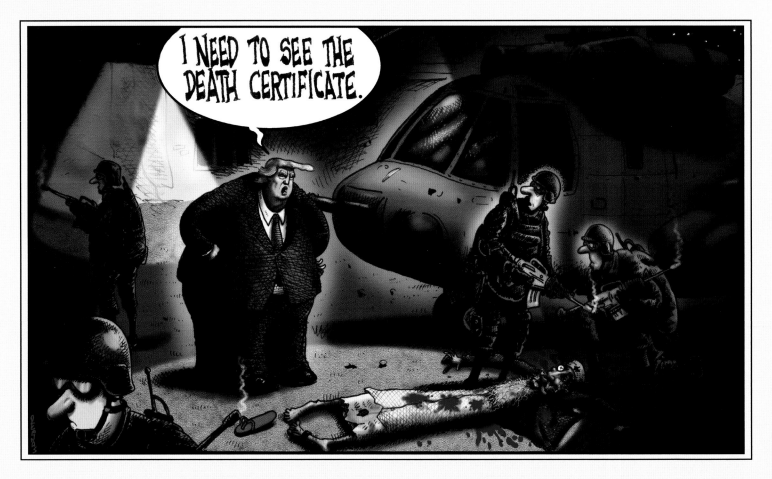

Donald Trump constantly questions the authenticity of Obama's birth certificate.

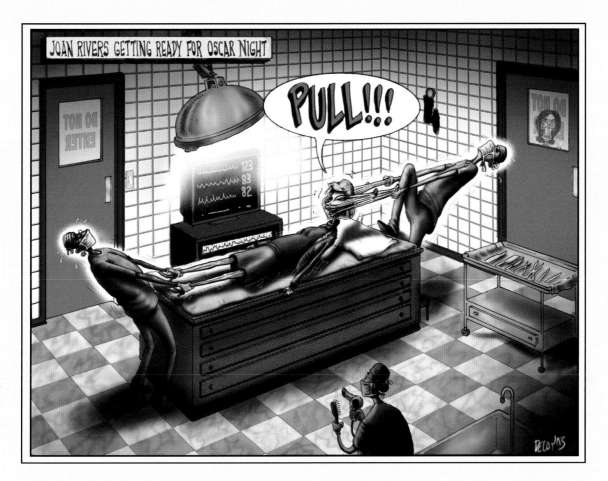

Joan Rivers has had one too many face lifts.

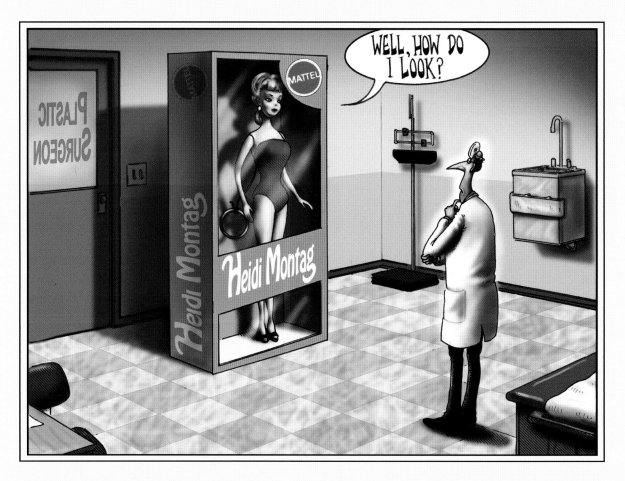

Reality star Heidi Montag considered to be addicted to plastic surgery.

CRIME

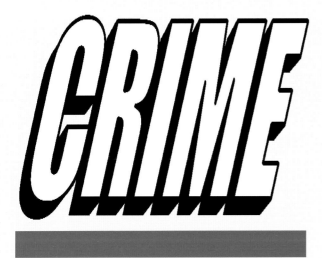

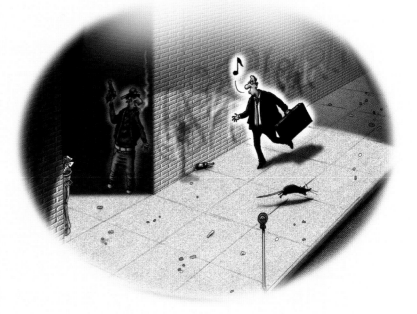

IT ONLY WORKS WITH 3-D PRINTERS.
ONE WAY

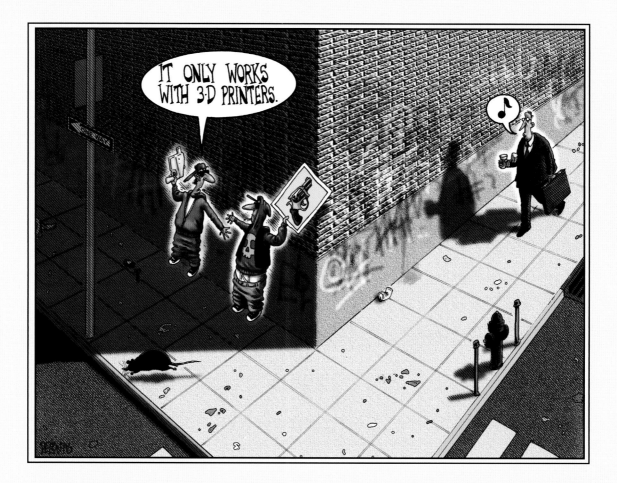

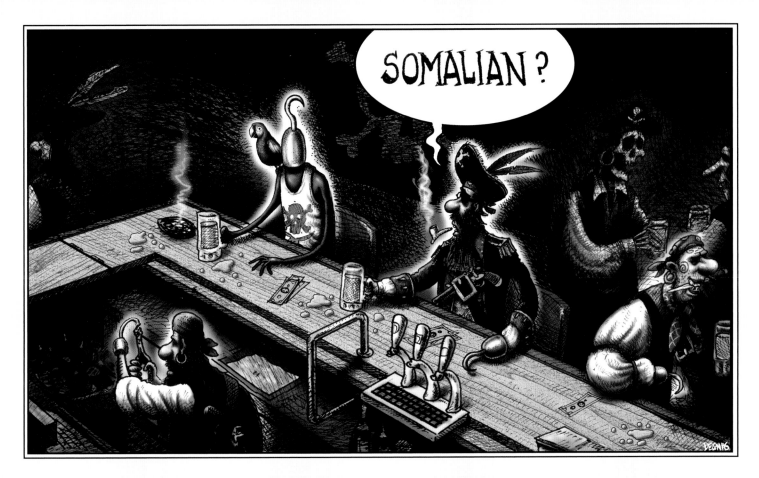

Somali pirates shot in the head by Navy Seal snipers.

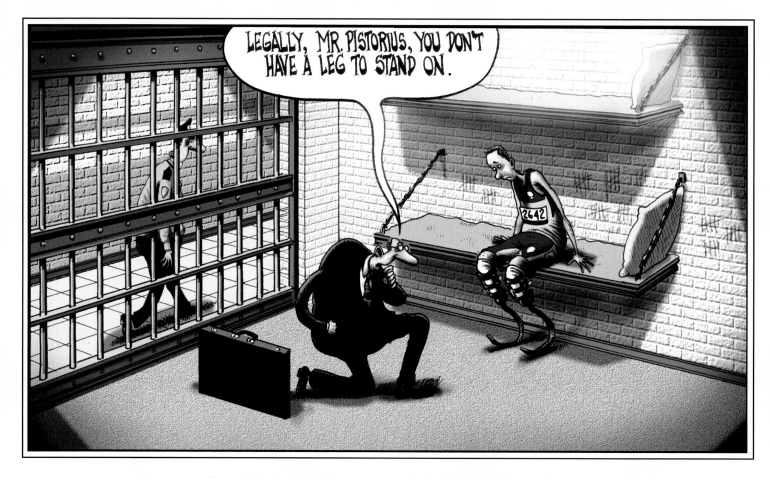

Legless athlete Oscar Pistorius arrested for murdering his girlfriend.

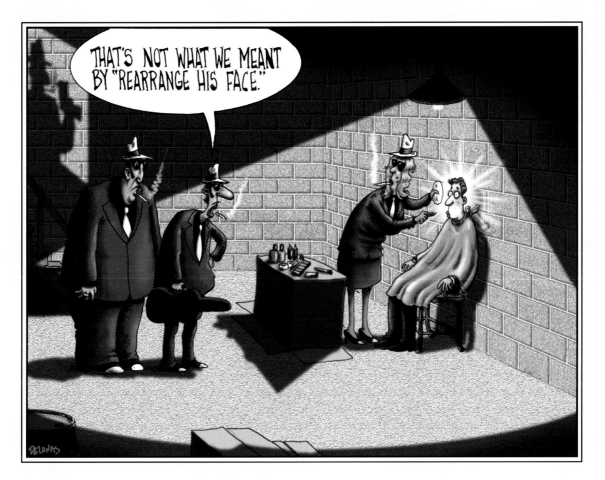

Women playing a bigger role in the mafia.

PARENTS' REACTIONS TO WOMEN TEACHERS HAVING SEX WITH THEIR STUDENTS.
3-E

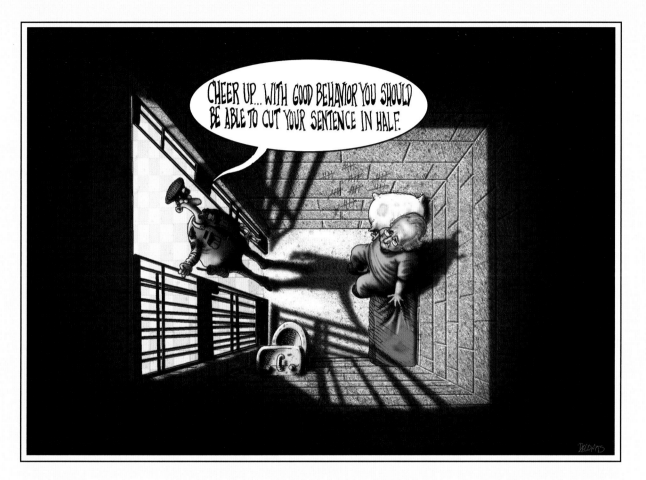

Bernie Madoff sentenced to 150 years.

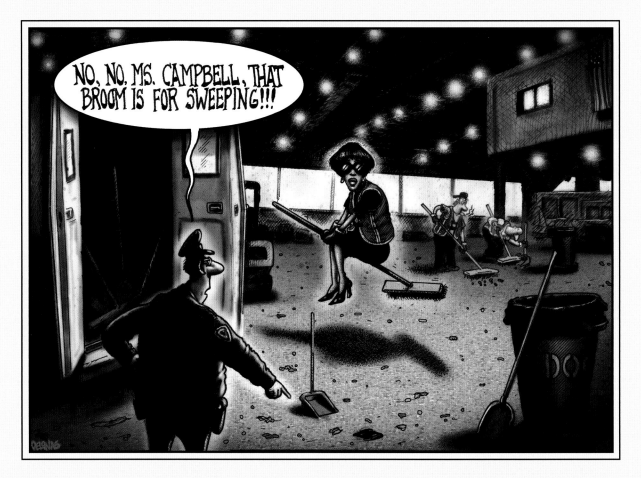

Naomi Campbell sentenced to community service for assaulting her maid.

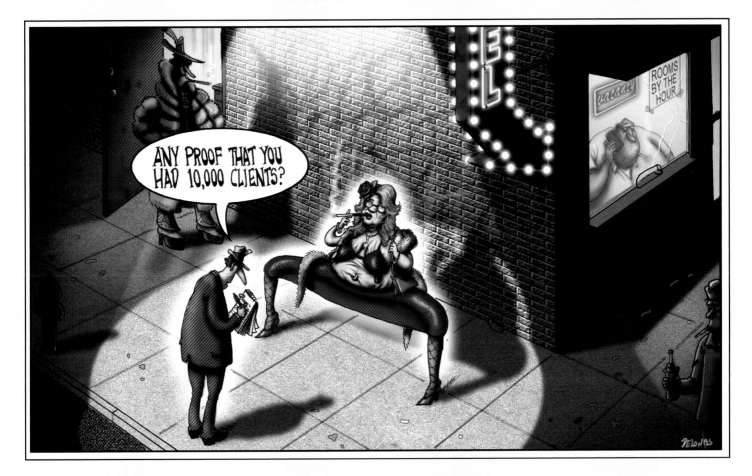

Prostitute Kristen Davis claims she had over 10,000 clients.

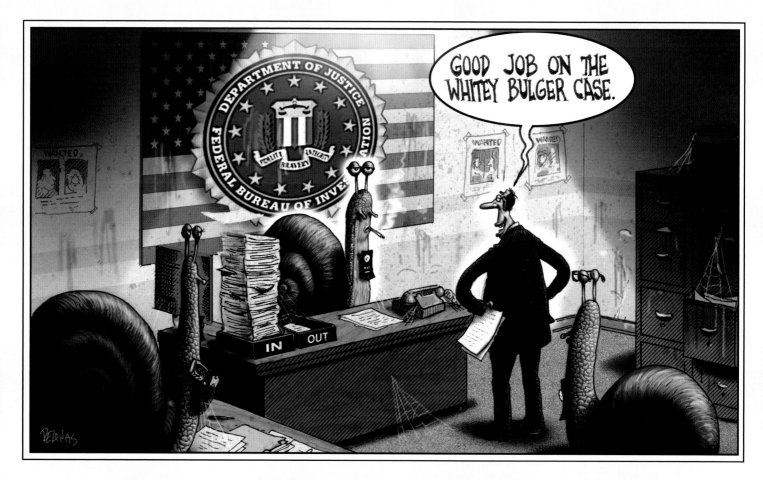

It took the FBI sixteen years to capture Whitey Bulger.

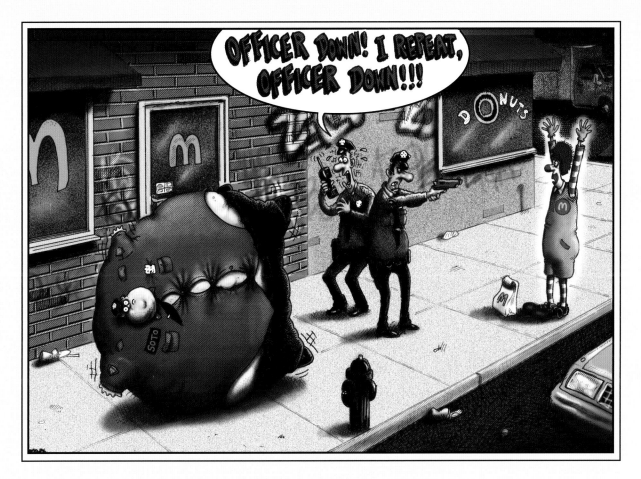

Five-hundred-pound police officer, Paul Soto.

POP CULTURE

Happy Holidays
KWANZAA
Season
SANTA, I THINK WE'RE GETTING A LITTLE CARRIED AWAY WITH THIS POLITICAL CORRECTNESS...

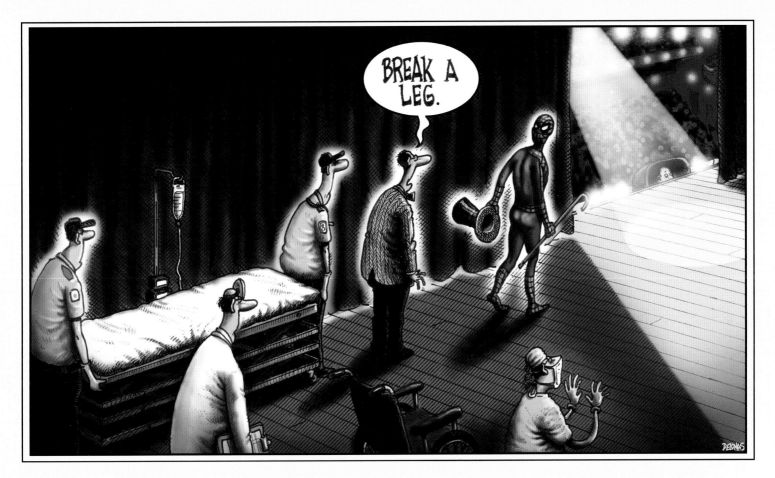

"Spiderman" on Broadway plagued by cast injuries.

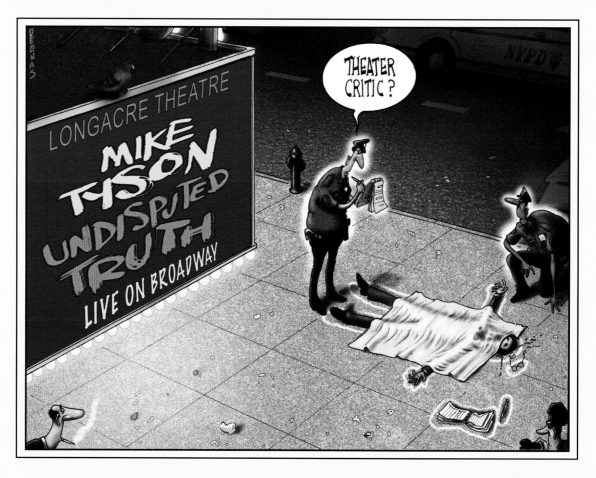

Mike Tyson's "Undisputed Truth" opens on Broadway.

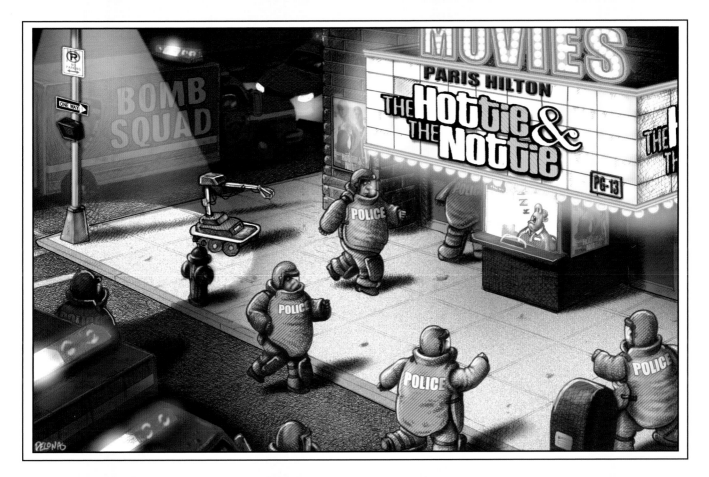

One of the all-time best movies.

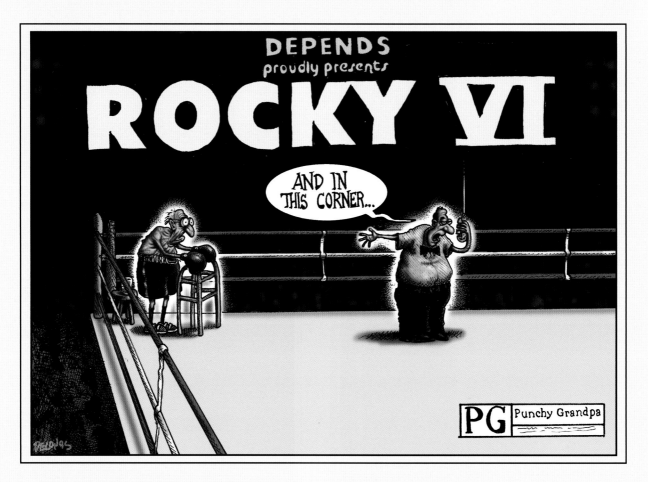

Sylvester Stallone considers making another Rocky movie.

HURRY UP, LEFTY. THE "SOPRANOS" IS ABOUT TO START.
CEMENT

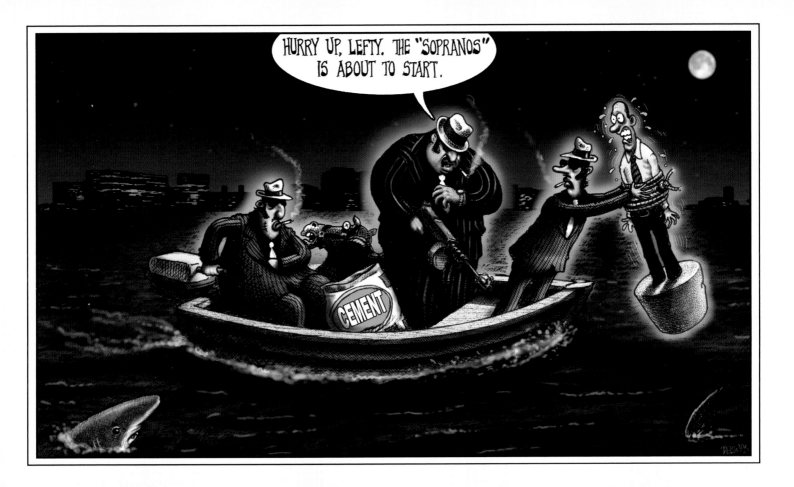

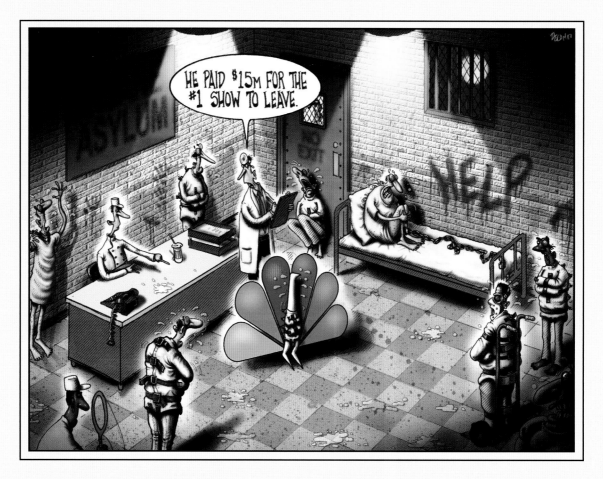

NBC pays Jay Leno to leave his #1-rated show.

THEY'RE FAIR... BUT ARE THEY BALANCED?
FOX NEWS Channel
BILL O'REILLY ACCUSED OF SEXUAL HARASSMENT BY HIS FORMER PRODUCER, ANDREA MAKRIS

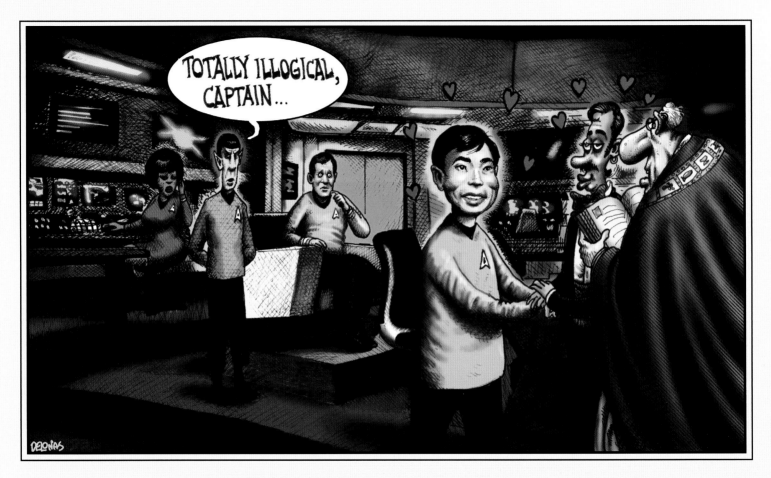

Star Trek's George Takei (Mr. Sulu) marries long-time boyfriend, Brad Altman.

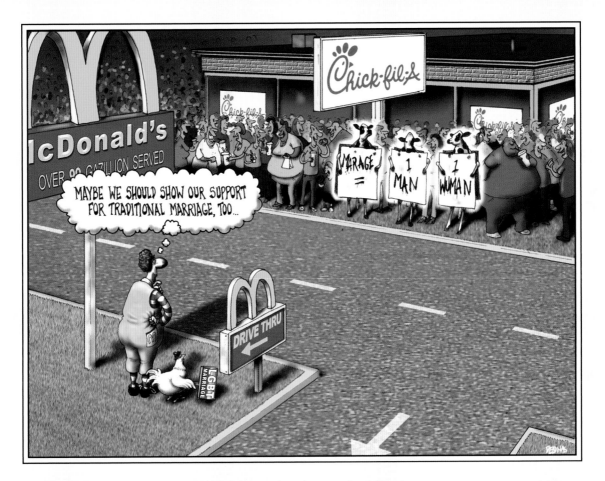

The Chic-Fil-A boycott backfires.

HIGHLIGHTS FROM THE GAY MARCH ON WASHINGTON D.C.
NOT MUCH FARTHER MEN!!!

CASTING THE FIRST STONE...
LGBT
GAY MARRIAGE
OUT OF THE WAY!!! YOU'RE BLOCKING MY SHOT!!!

WE USED THIS TO DISPERSE THE PROTESTERS.
JOB FAIR
APPLICATIONS
DOWN WITH THE 1%
TAX THE RICH
ARE THE 99%
OWS
SHARE THE WEALTH

MOM, DAD... THEY KICKED US OUTTA ZUCCOTTI PARK, SO I NEED TO OCCUPY YOUR HOUSE AGAIN.
DELONAS

THEY GOT AHOLD OF MY "NAUGHTY AND NICE" LIST.
WikiLeaks
Diary
Support Us
About Us
Submenu

WONDER WHAT SANTA IS GONNA BRING ME THIS YEAR?
DEMS

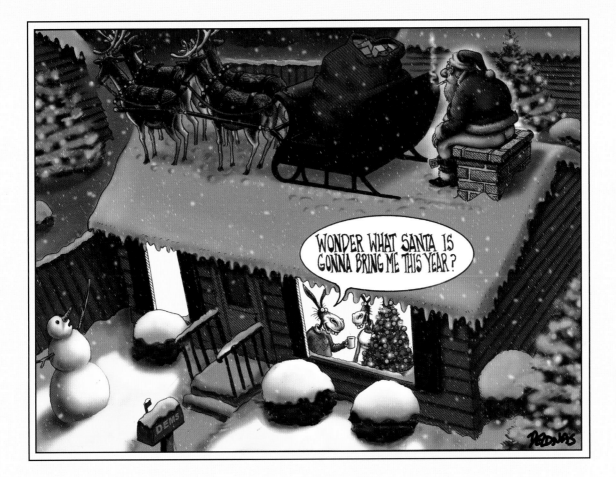

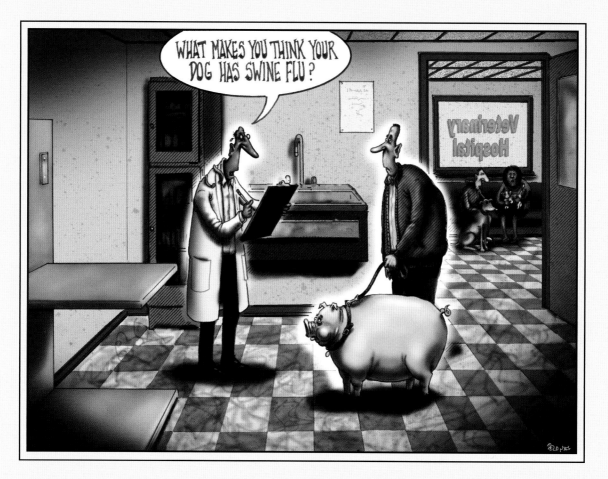

Swine Flu, H1N1, effects pets as well as people.

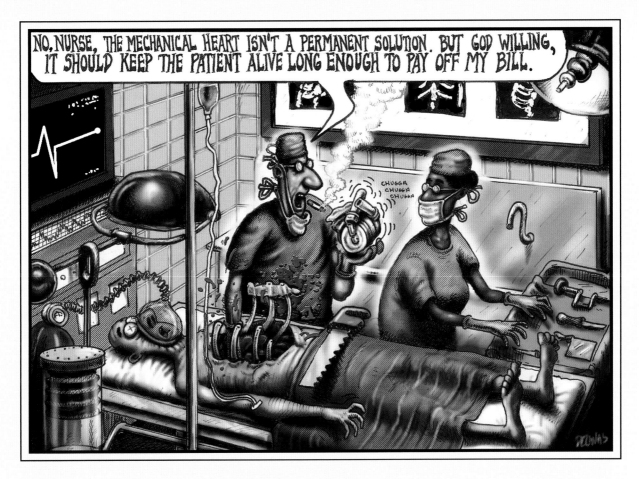

Artificial heart gives hope to many.

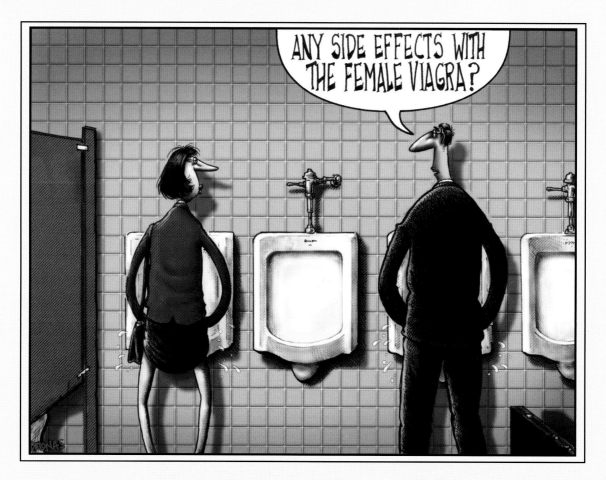

Women taking Viagra report mild side effects.

TRANSEXUAL THOMAS BEATIE GIVES BIRTH
IT'S A BOY!!!
WHAT ABOUT THE BABY?
Maternity Ward

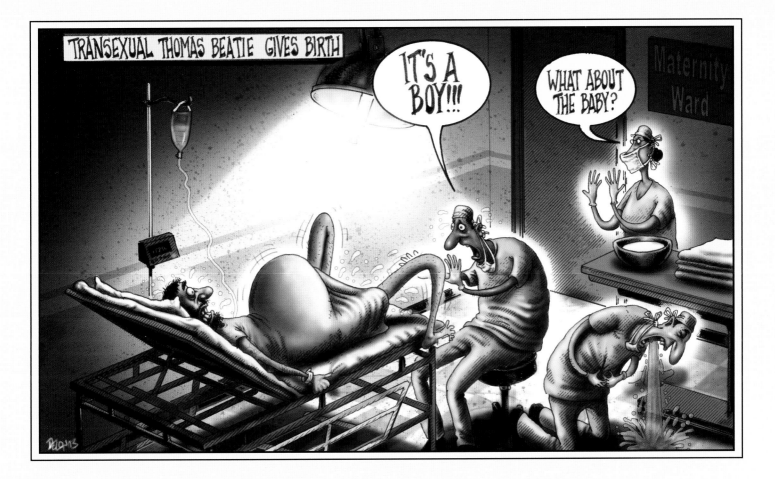

THE DOCTOR WILL SEE YOU NOW.
Veteran's Hospital
Waiting Room

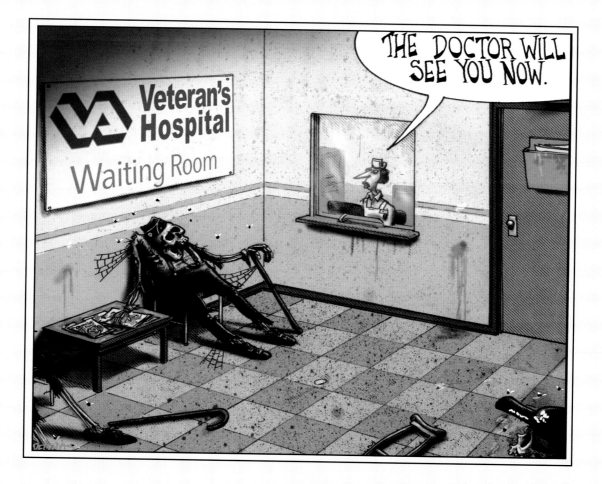

MY WALLET LOST A LITTLE WEIGHT.
Weight Watchers
Slim Fast

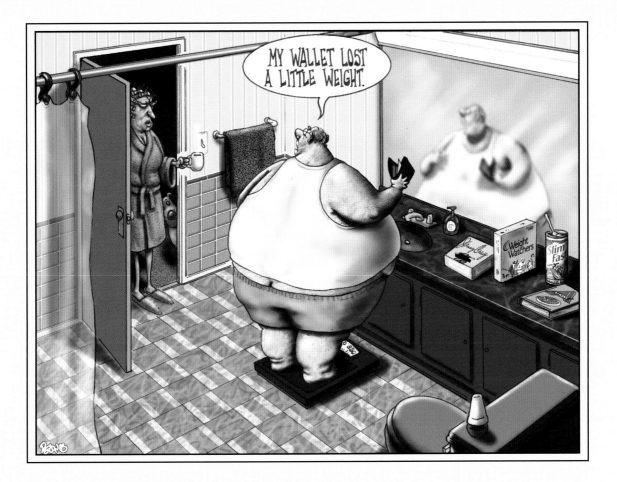

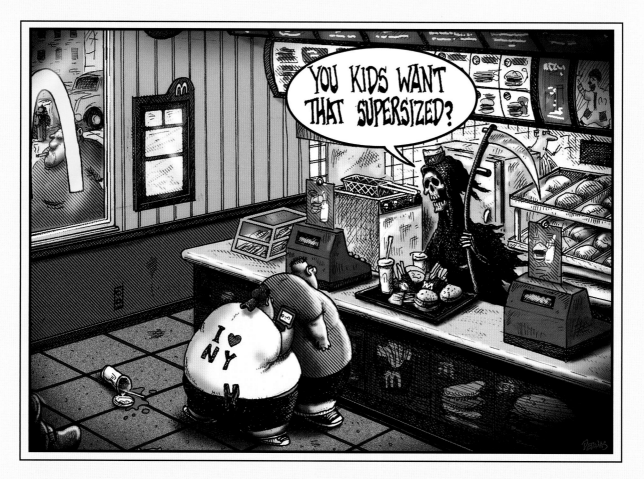

Obesity epidemic among children.

TRUMP UNIVE
INTRO TO PRE-NUPS
COMB OVERS 101
DATING YOUNGER WOMEN 201
THE ART OF THE GIANT EGO
T

Donald Trump creates Trump University, which is later charged with illegal business practices.

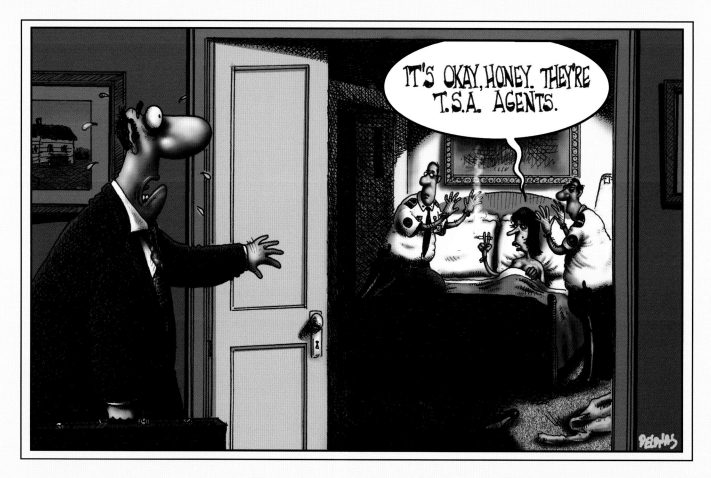

Overly invasive body searchers by TSA agents.

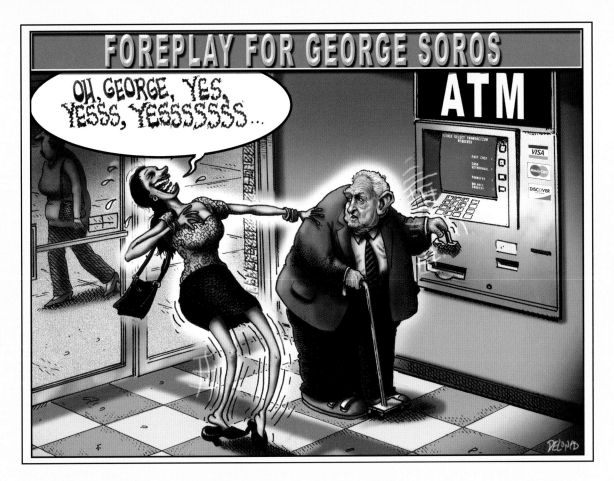

Octogenarian billionaire George Soros dating younger women in their twenties and early thirties.

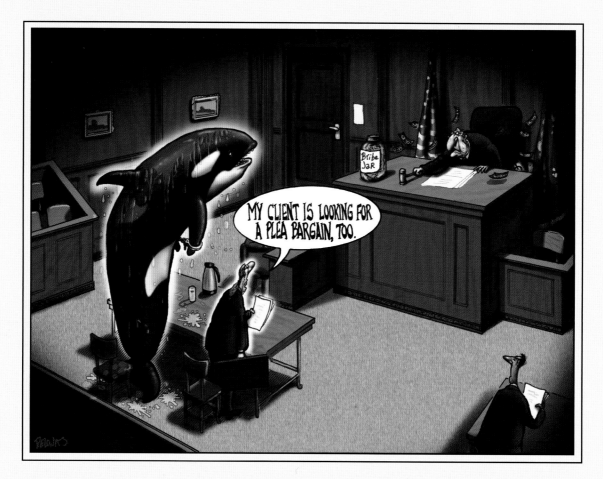

Orlando's SeaWorld orca kills trainer.

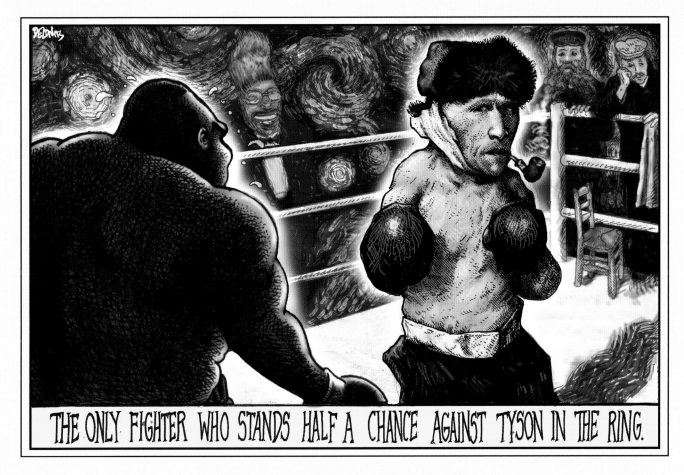

Mike Tyson bites off part of Evander Holyfield's ear.

NY / NJ

BLOOMBERG
ANY BANS FOR TODAY, YOUR HIGHNESS?

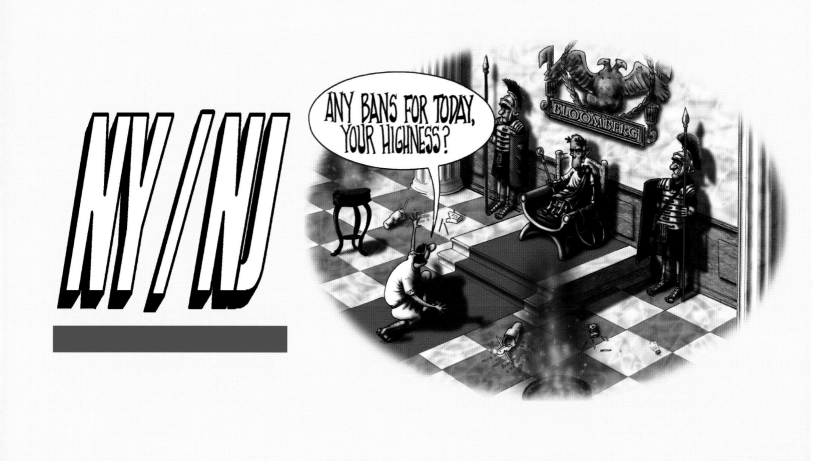

SEE, I TOLD YUH WE COULD AFFORD TO LIVE IN MANHATTAN.
SOLD

Manhattan rents soar.

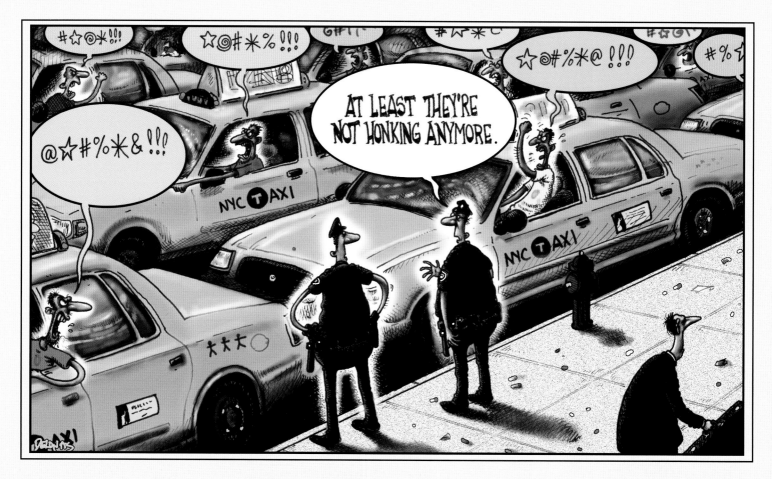

NYC orders cab drivers to stop honking their horns.

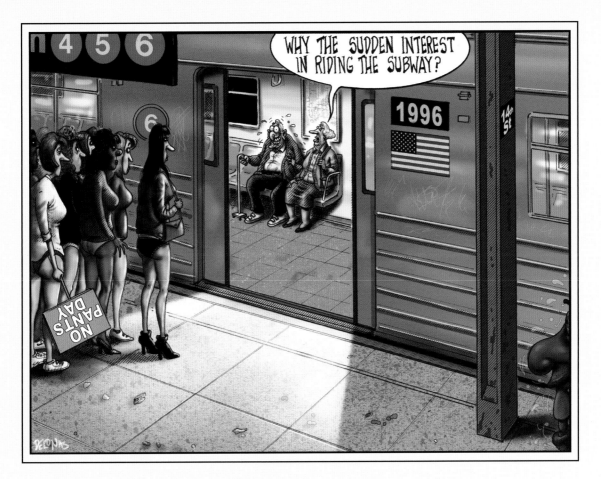

NYC's annual "No Pants Day" subway ride.

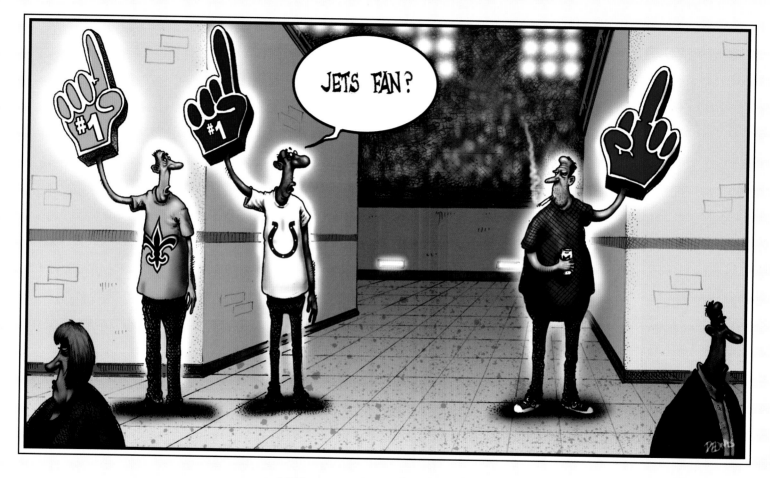

NY Jets not going to the Super Bowl.

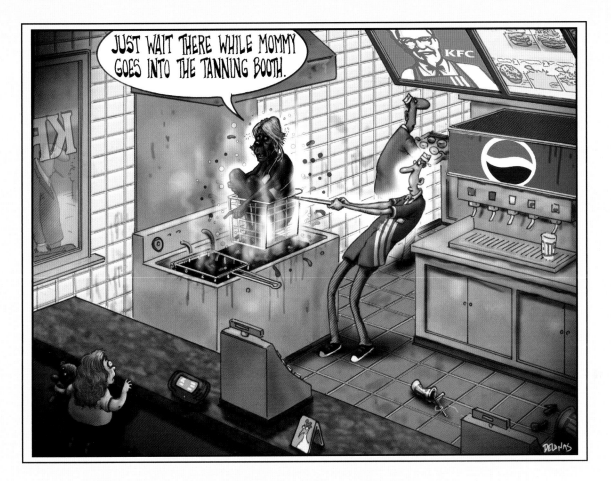

NJ tanning mom, Patricia Krentcil.

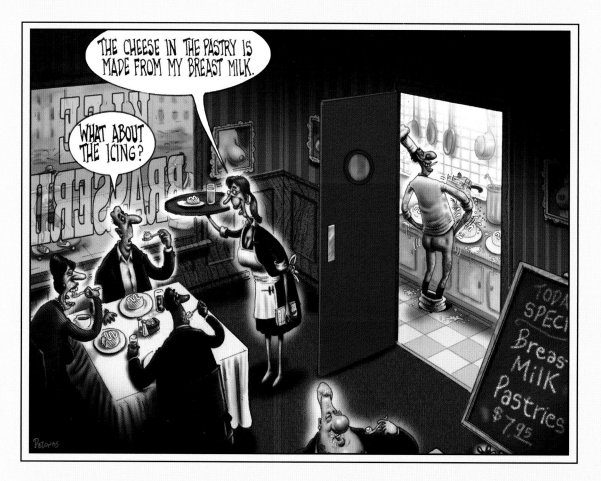

Klee Brassier restaurant makes its cheese pastries from human breast milk.

NYC SANITATION
YOU KNOW WHAT WE DO TO SNITCHES?
PELONAS

The Sanitation Department is criticized for inadequate response to snow storm.

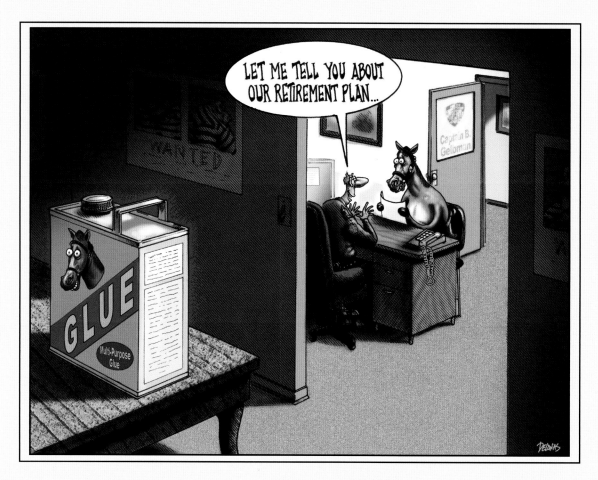

NYPD horse retirement plan criticized.

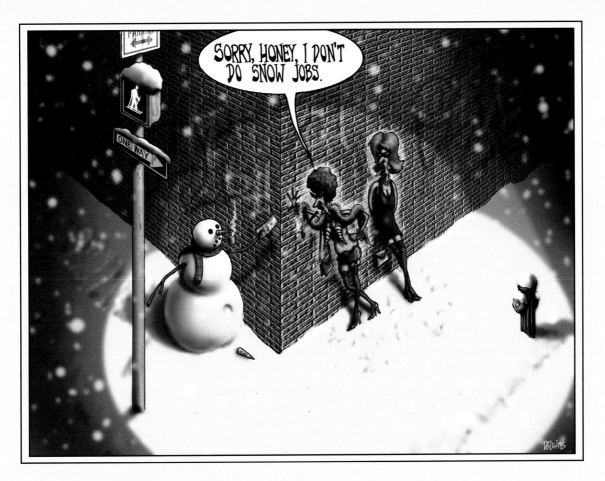

Governor Jim McGreevey resigns after admitting he's gay.

GOV. ANDREW CUOMO LOOKS FOR A NEW LOGO TO REPLACE "I ♥ NY"
MUCH BETTER.
I NY
TAX-PAYER
I ♥ NY

LIBERAL POLICY
SIZE MATTERS!!!
NO
16oz SODAS
WEINER
FOR
MAYOR

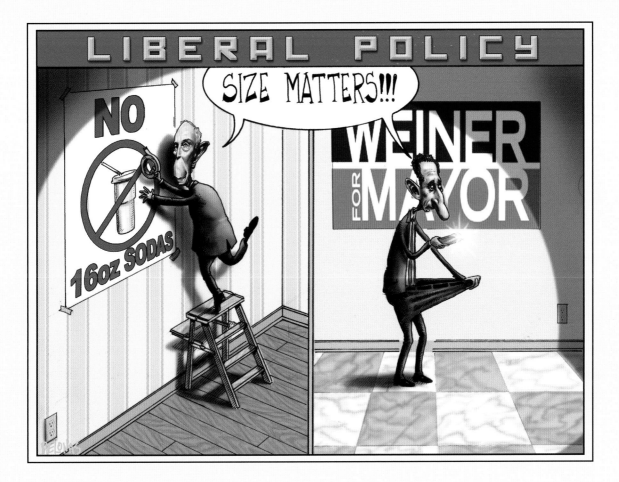

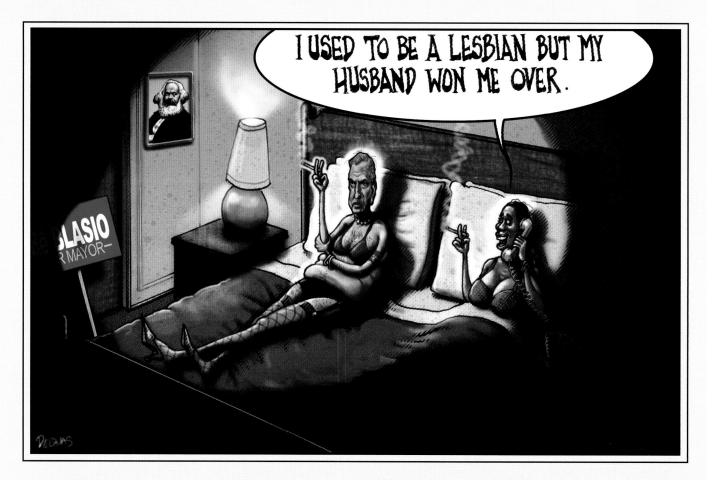

Mayor Bill de Blasio's wife was a lesbian.

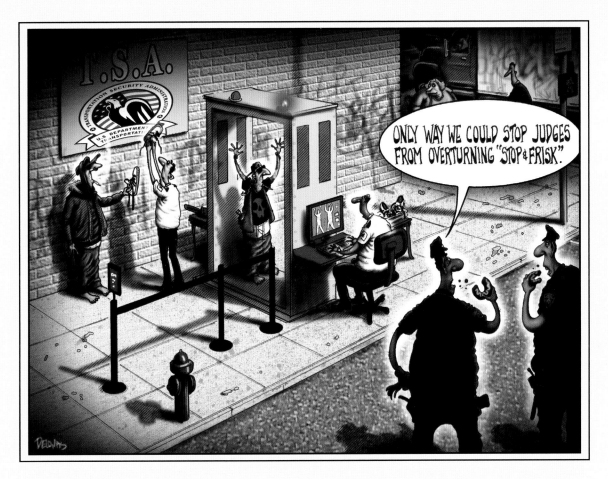

The NYPD's "Stop-and-Frisk" program raises concerns over violations of citizen's civil rights.

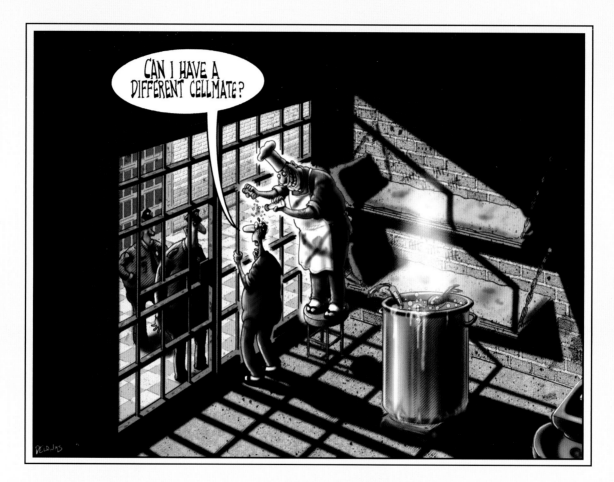

NYC cannibal cop, Gilbert Valle.

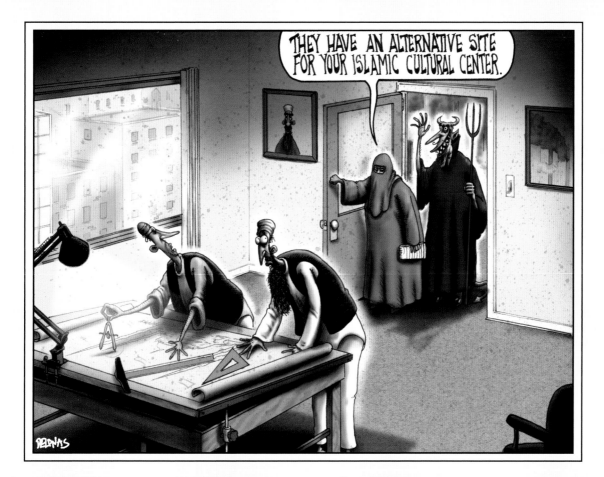

Alternate sites suggested for Ground Zero Mosque.

DESIGN COMPETITION FOR THE NEW WORLD TRADE CENTER AT GROUND ZERO
INTERESTING DESIGN... I ASSUME IT'LL BE FACING MECCA ?

THE FREEDOM TOWER SURPASSES HEIGHT OF EMPIRE STATE BUILDING
BUILDING ENVY?

THEY CAN JUST ASK ME ABOUT IT.
...OR ME.
ME TOO.
DITTO.
Q: ISLAM
A: You deserve to know
877-WHY-ISLAM
DELONAS

1-877-WHY-ISLAM ad campaign.

SUSHI
RESTAURANT
I ASK FOR TOLERANCE.
Pearl Harbor
Memorial
GRAND
OPENING
DARNAS

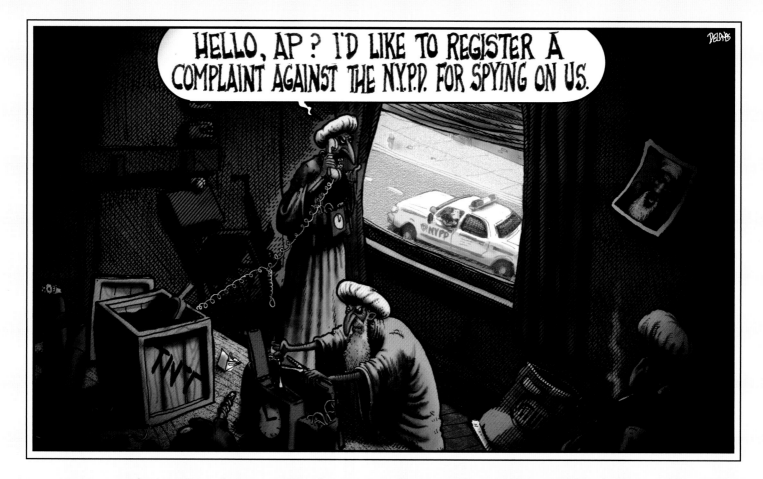

The Associated Press exposes the NYPD's spying program in Muslim neighborhoods.

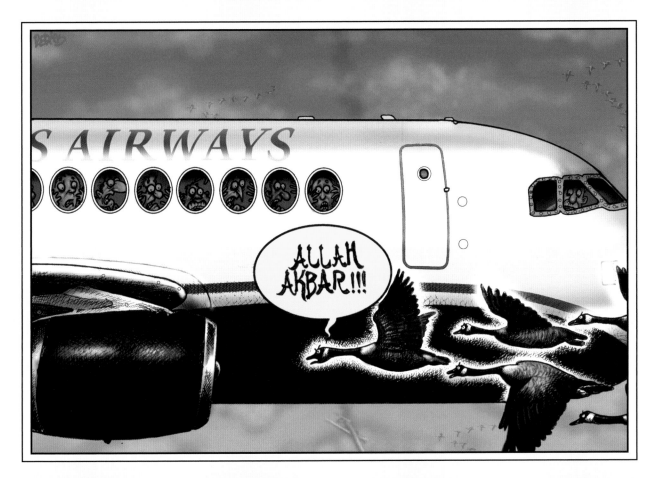

US Airways Flight 1549 loses engine power after running into a flock of Canadian geese and splash lands into the icy Hudson.

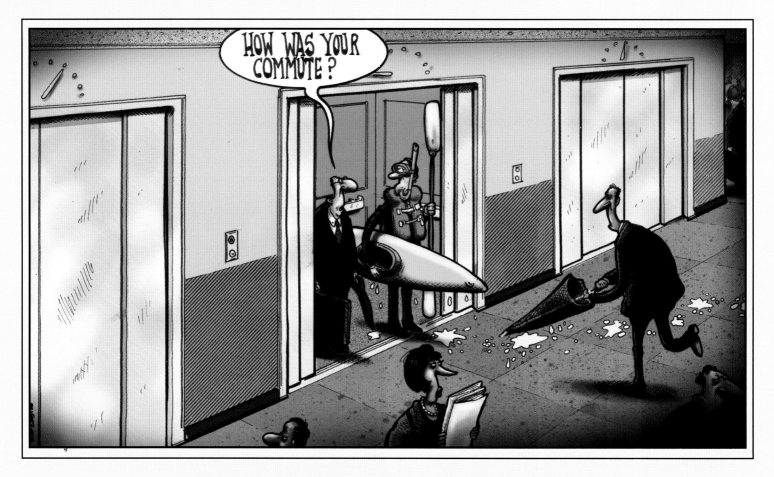

Hurricane Sandy floods NY.

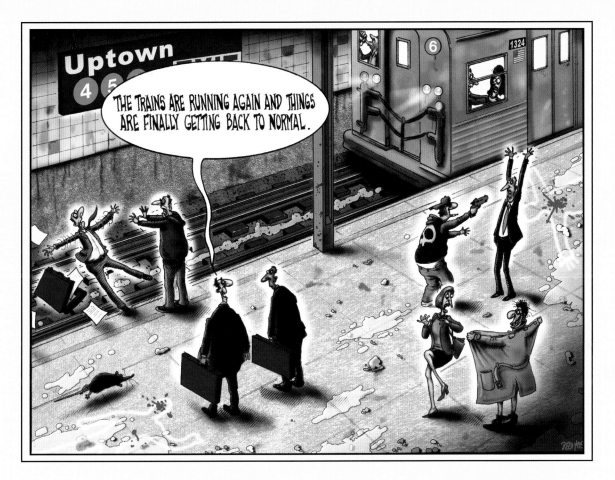

The water recedes and the subways are running again after Hurricane Sandy.

POLITICS

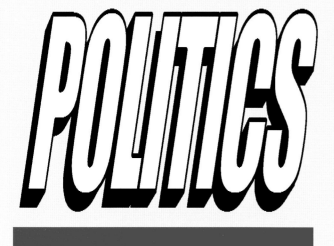

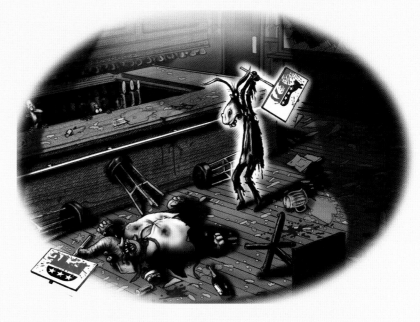

FOOL, FETCH ME A TAXPAYER!!!
BIG GOV'T
DELONAS

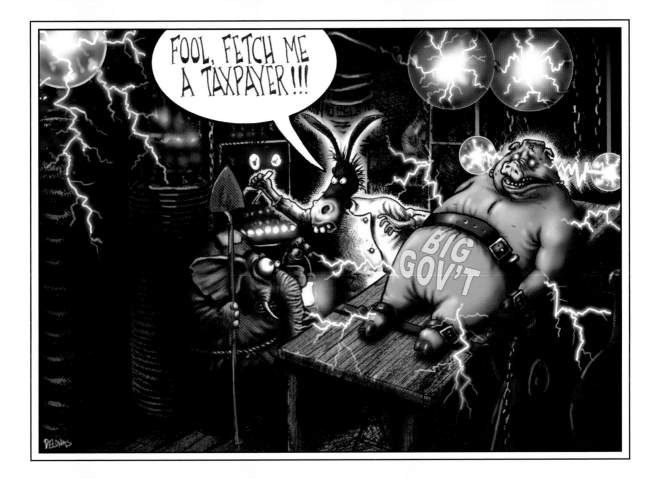

STIMULATE.
BERNANKE
ECONOMY

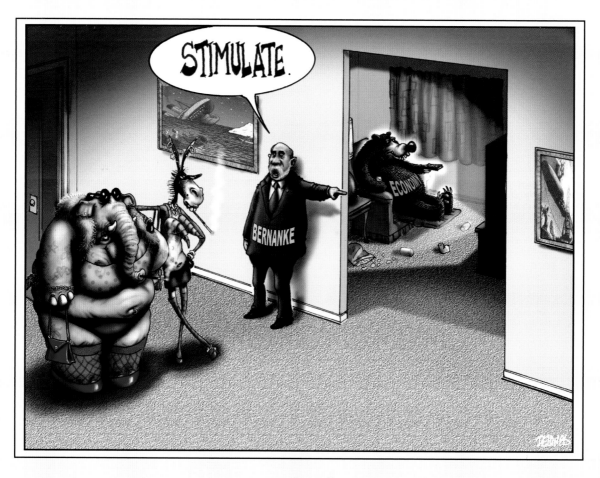

Stimulas Bill.

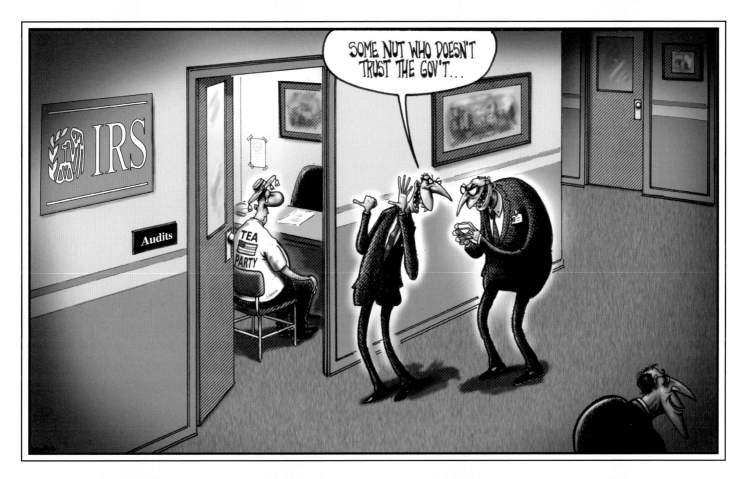

IRS targets political groups like the Tea Party.

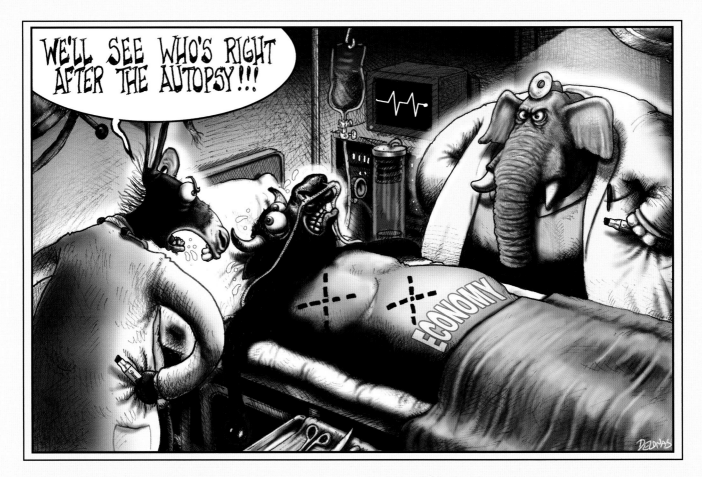

Political differences on the best way to deal with the economic crisis.

GOVERNMENT WORKERS
SEEMS LIKE THEY'RE ALREADY SHUTDOWN.
CIVIL SERVICE
neither civil, nor a service
Ask us if we care
NEXT WINDOW
NEXT WINDOW
NEXT WINDOW

Government shutdown.

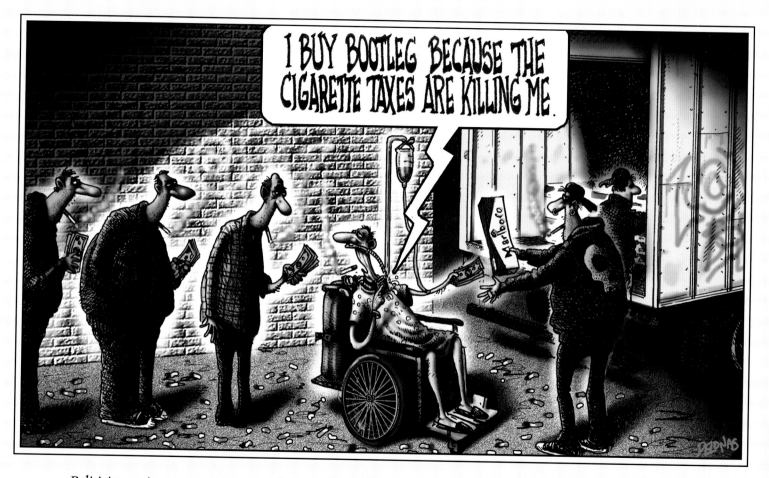

Politicians raise taxes on cigarettes claiming that will convince smokers to quit. Instead, it creates a demand for bootleg cigarettes.

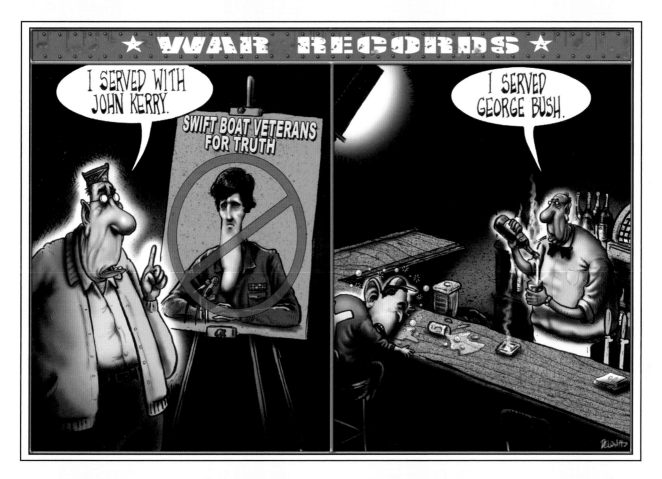

Kerry accused of lying about his military service, and Bush accused of being a former alcoholic.

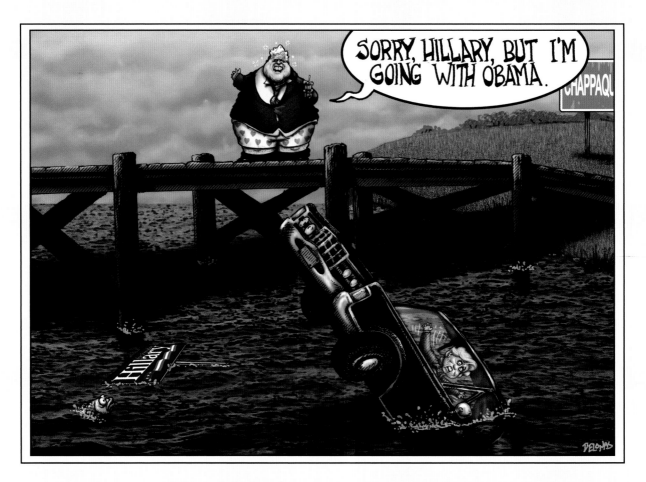

Ted Kennedy backs Obama in 2008 Democrat primaries.

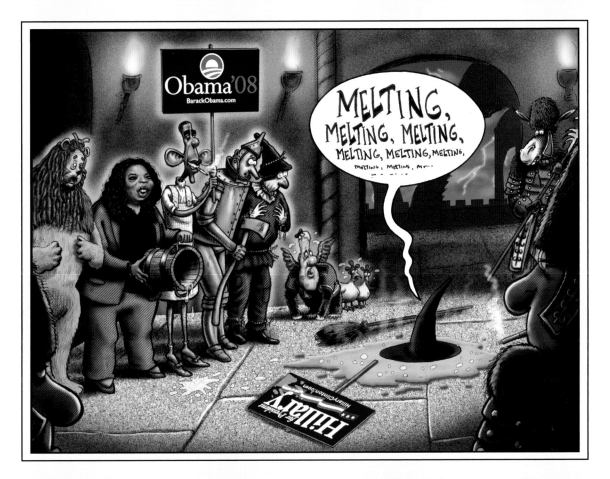

Oprah's endorsement of Obama leads to Hillary's 2008 presidential campaign collapsing.

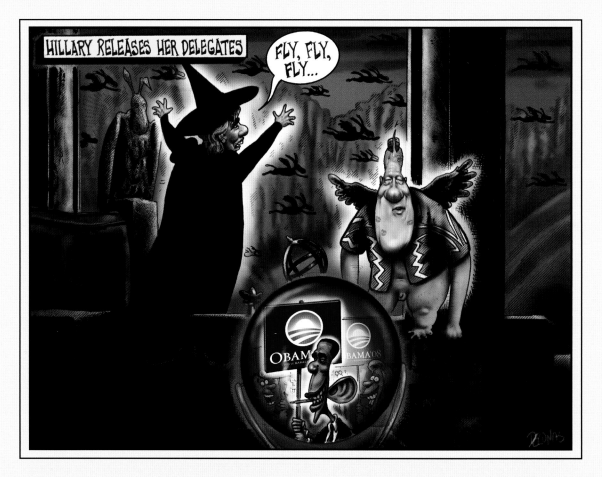

Hillary drops out of the race, releasing her delegates.

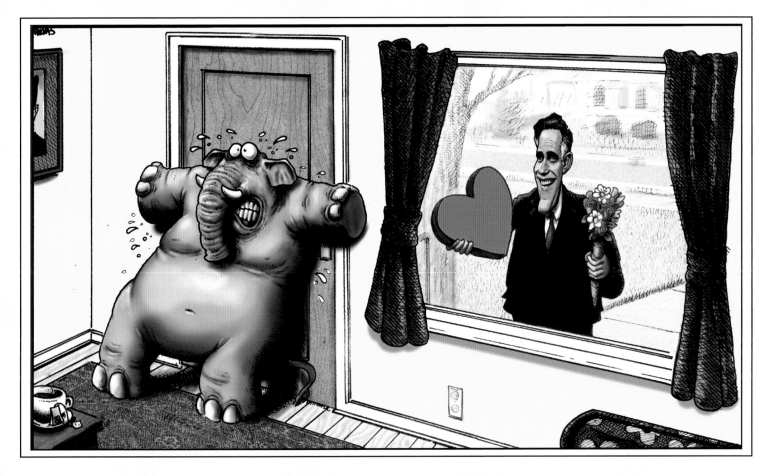

Mitt Romney leading in the GOP primaries.

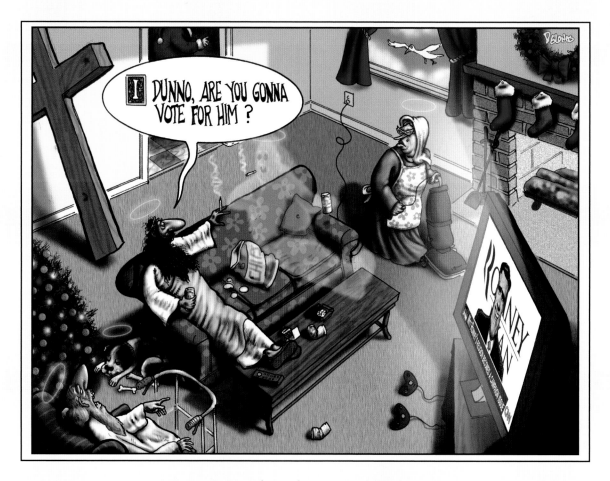

Mitt Romney's religion becomes a campaign issue.

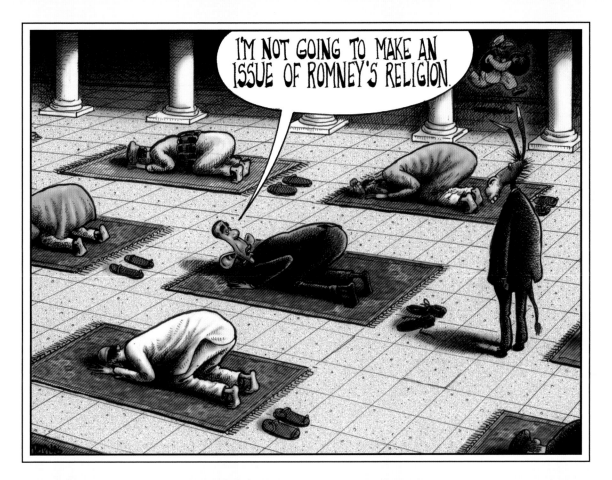

Democrats keep bringing up Romney's religion, but what about Obama's?

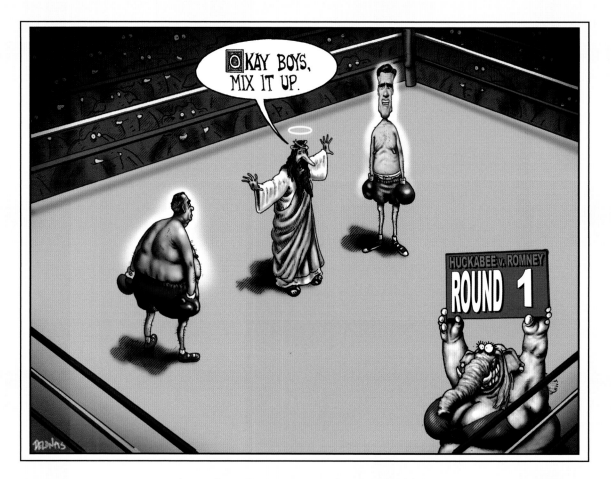

Religion becomes an issue in the GOP primaries.

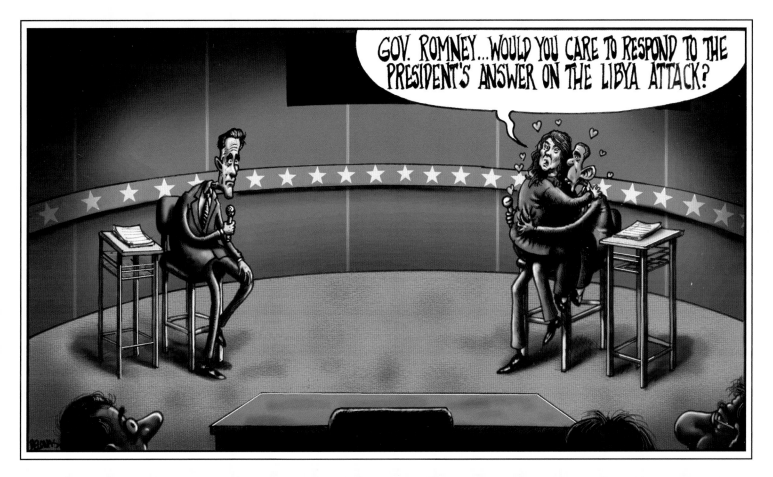

CNN's Candy Crowley is clearly not a neutral moderator.

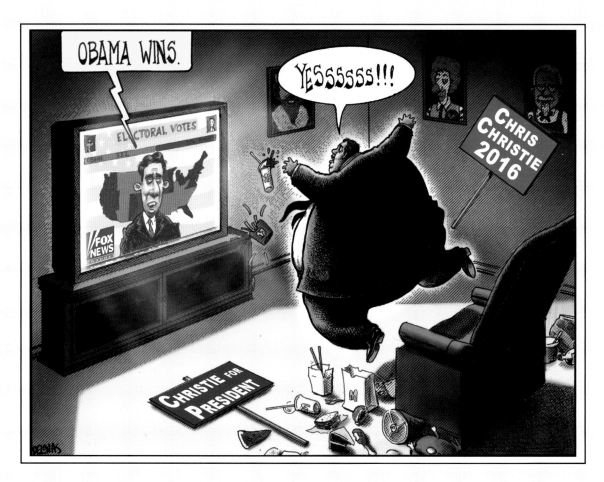

Poor Governor Christie—he wanted so badly for Romney to win.

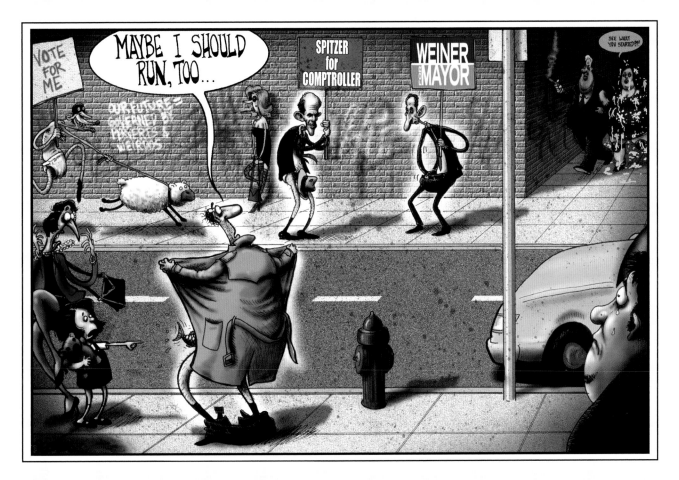

Spitzer and Weiner try to make political comebacks.

AT LEAST I GOT LAID, SEÑOR DANGER.
VOTE SPITZER 2013

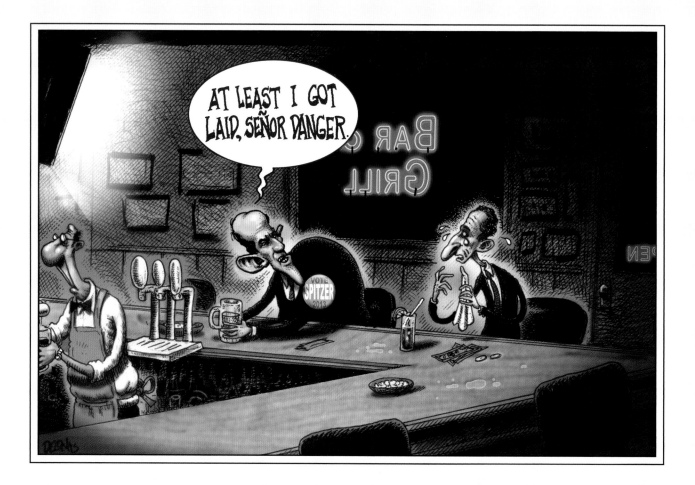

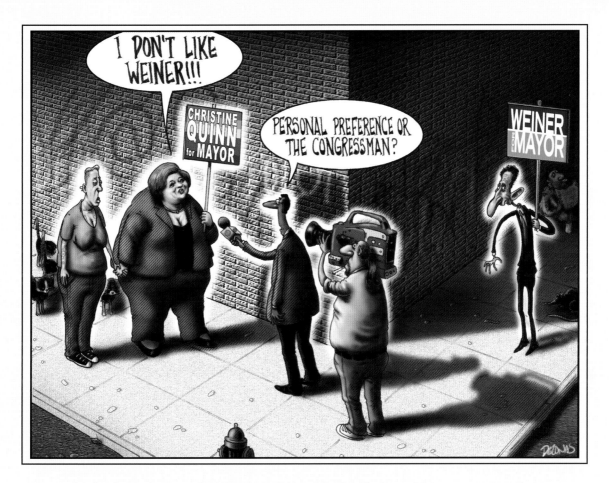

Mayoral candidate Christine Quinn is unhappy with Anthony Weiner entering the race.

START THE TRANSFUSION.
ECONOMY
OBAMA CARE

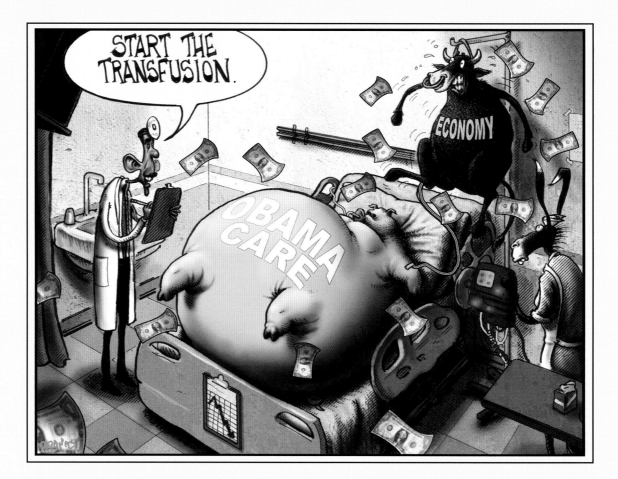

OBAMA CARE

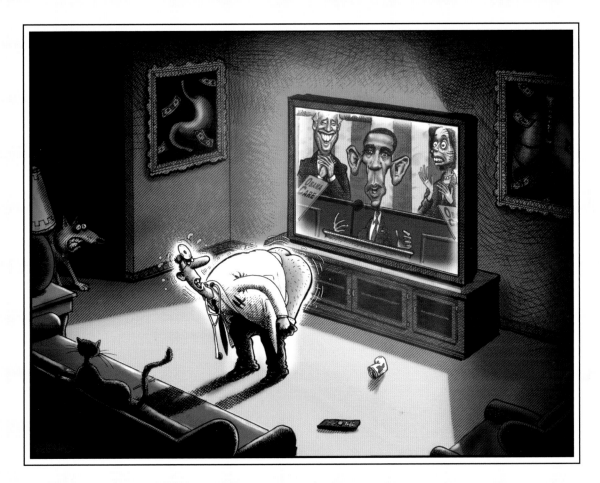

Reaction to ObamaCare.

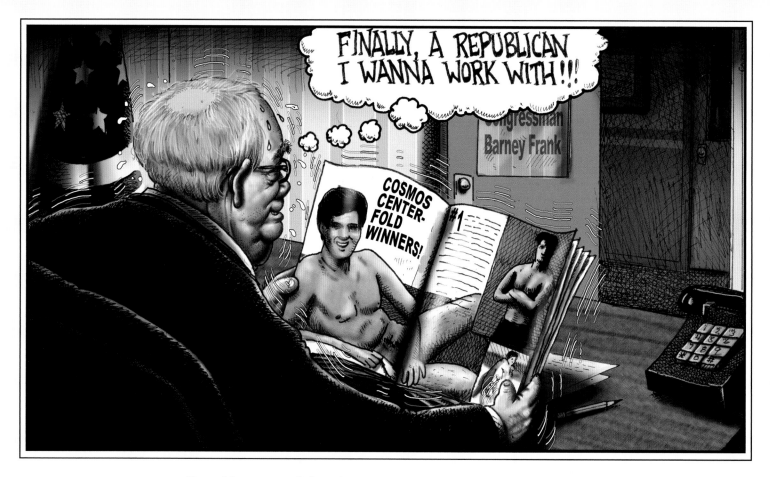

Republican candidate Scott Brown posed naked for Cosmo.

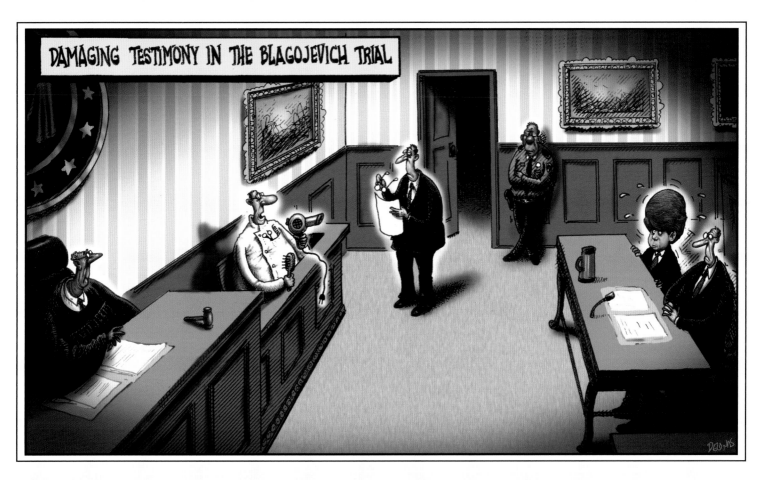

Governor Blagojevich on trial for trying to sell Obama's old senate seat.

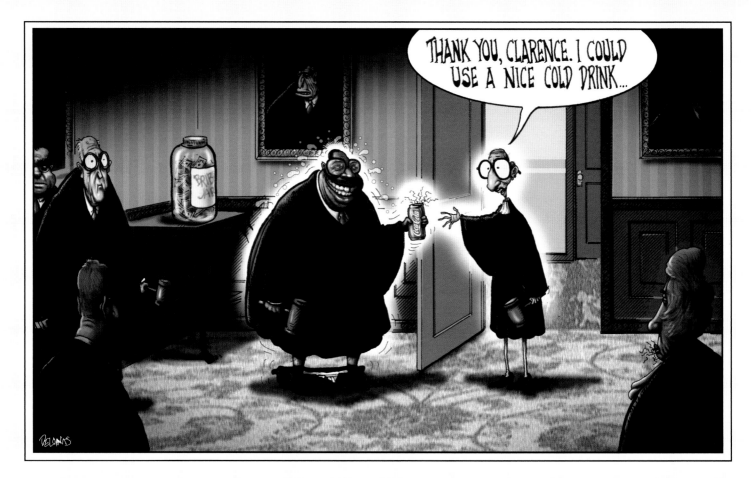

Ruth Ginsburg confirmed to the Supreme Court.

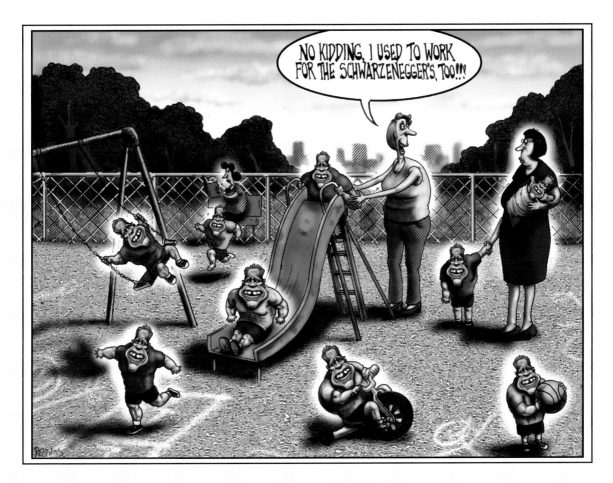

Schwarzenegger's infidelity.

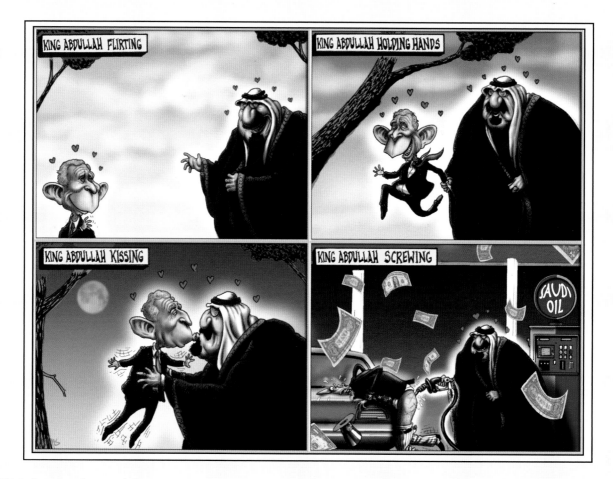

Bush publicly kissing the Saudi king was in poor taste, especially given Saudi Arabia's relationship to Al Qaeda and OPEC.

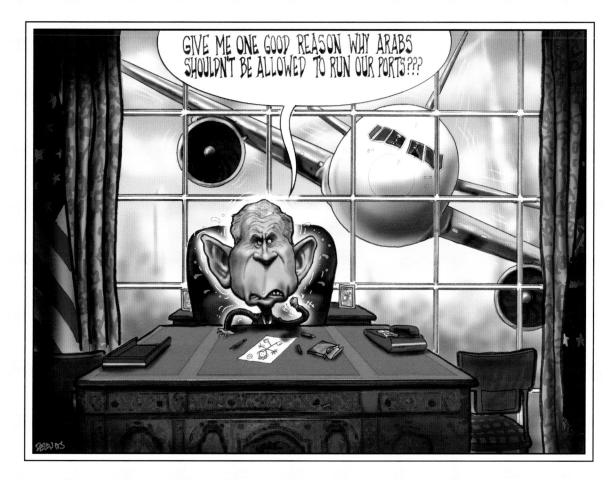

Bush defends the United Arab Emirates's plan to oversee six US ports.

PAY NO ATTENTION TO THE MAN BEHIND THE CURTAIN.
CHENEY
VICE PRESIDENT OF THE UNITED STATES

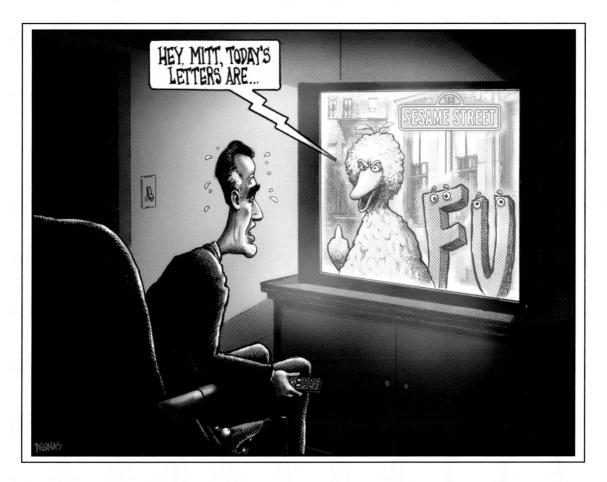

Romney evokes Big Bird while saying that we should cut funding for PBS.

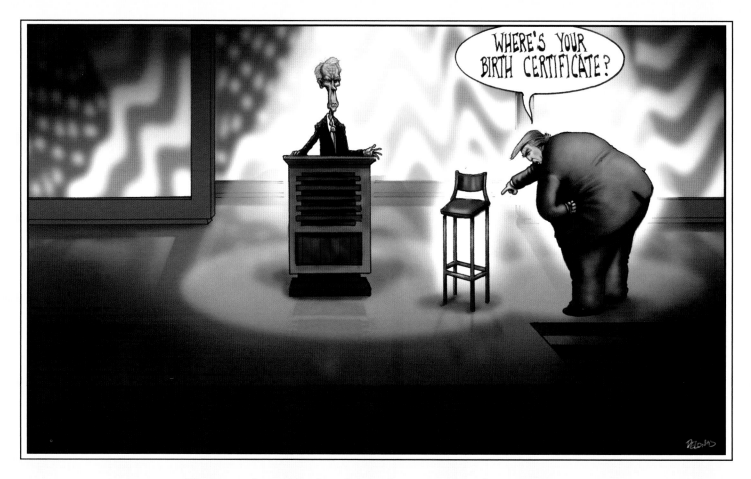

Clint's speech would've been better if Trump was in the routine, too.

PRESIDENTS

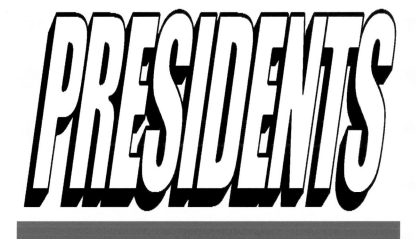

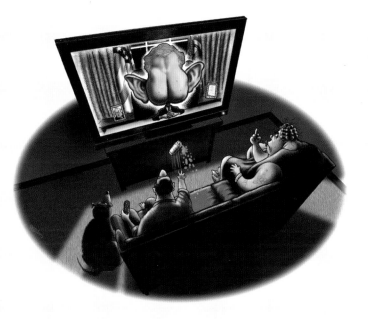

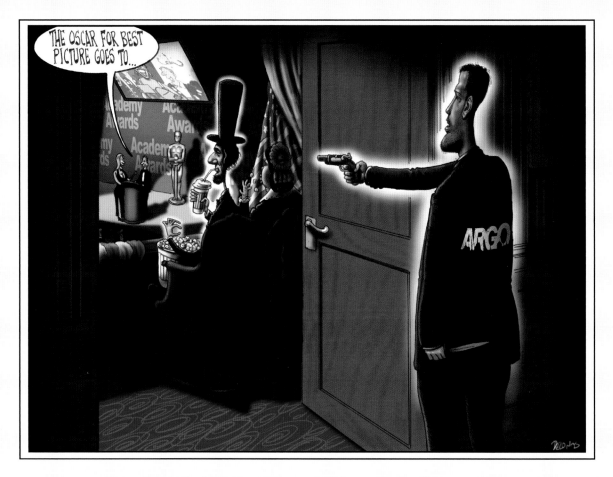

Lincoln *loses best picture to* Argo *at the Oscars.*

Memorable Presidential Quotes
I CAN NOT TELL A LIE.
YOU CAN'T FOOL ALL THE PEOPLE, ALL THE TIME.
THE ONLY THING WE HAVE TO FEAR, IS FEAR ITSELF.
ASK NOT WHAT YOUR COUNTRY CAN DO FOR YOU.
I DID NOT HAVE SEX WITH THAT WOMAN.
DELONAS

BILL PUTS THE FINISHING TOUCHES ON HIS BOOK
My Life
Bill Clinton
I Loved this book! -ML
I hated this book! -HRC
DELONAS

BILL, IF YOU DON'T MIND, LET ME HANG THE MISTLETOE.

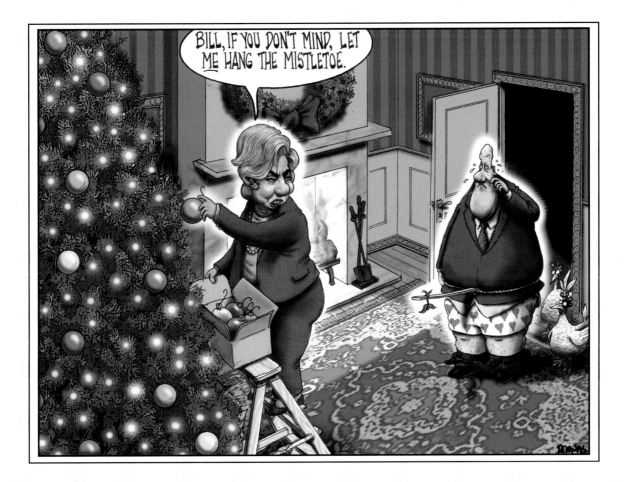

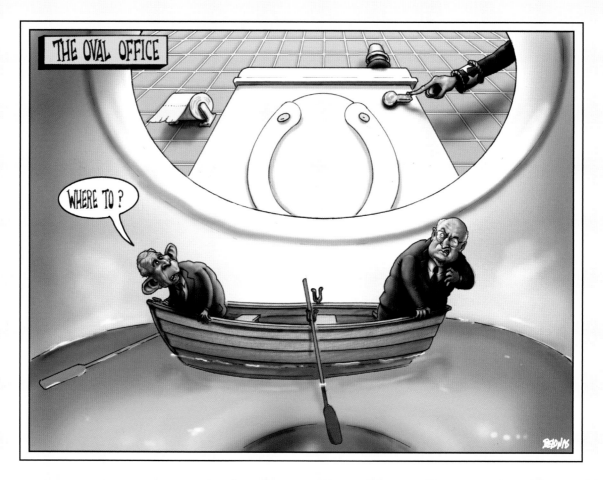

Bush's White House in trouble.

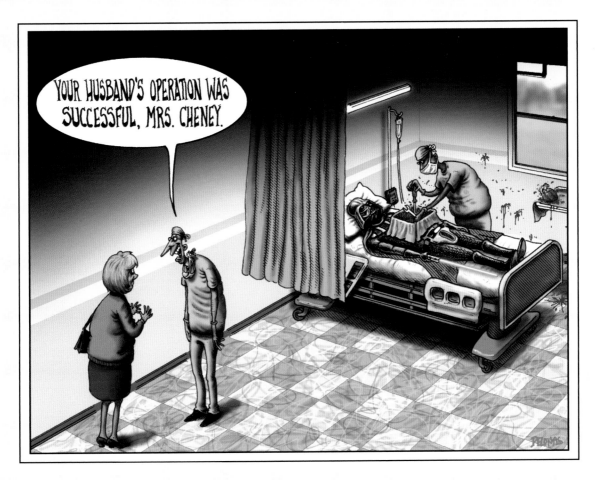

VP Dick Cheney's heart surgery.

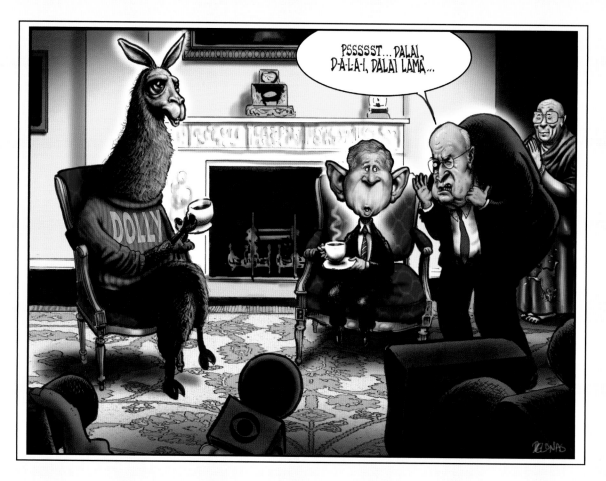

Bush meets with the Dalai Lama.

DELDARS
MISSION ACCOMPLISHED
HAPPY ANNIVERSARY...
IRAQ

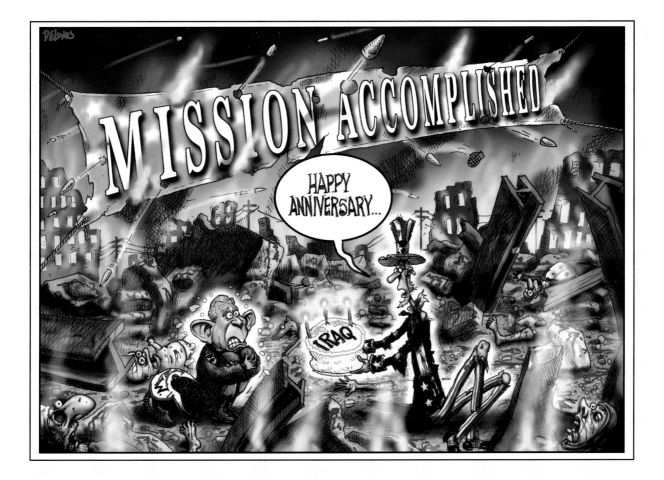

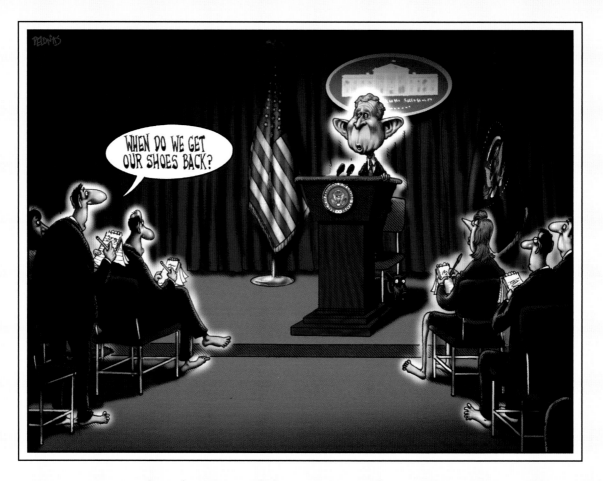

Shoes thrown at Bush during a press conference in Iraq.

FAREWELL...
DELONAS

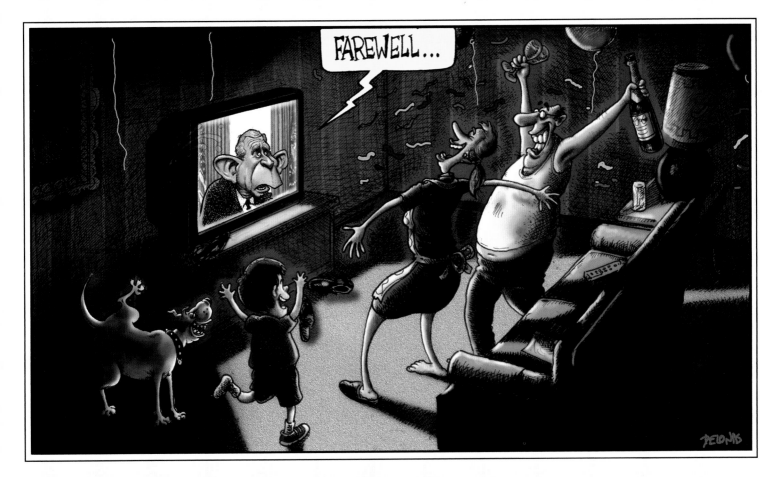

Bush leaves office.

OBAMA RELEASES MORE INFORMATION ON HIS BIRTH

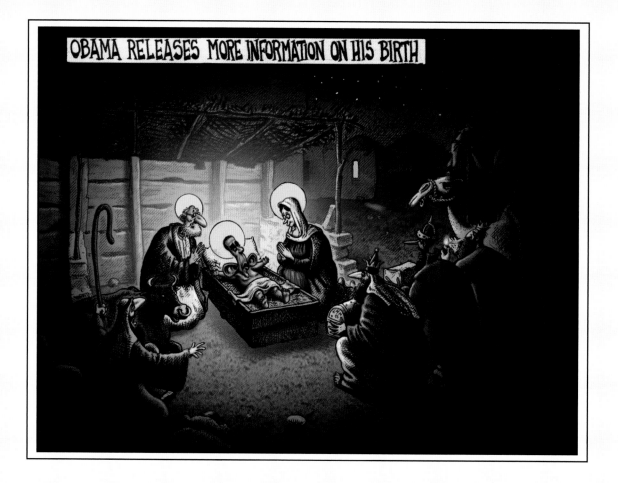

PROGRESSIVES
Proudly Present
OBAMA HOOD
TAX-
PAYER
R REDISTRIBUTION
SOME MATERIAL MAY BE INAPPROPRIATE FOR TAXPAYERS

NOW WHERE TO?
DETROIT
DEMOCRAT POLICIES

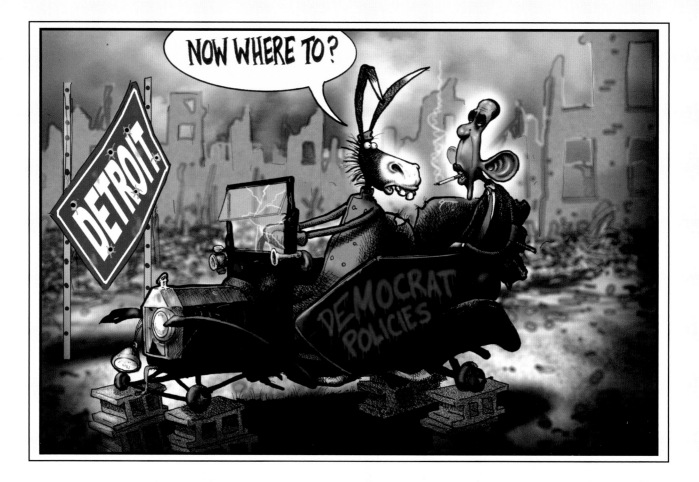

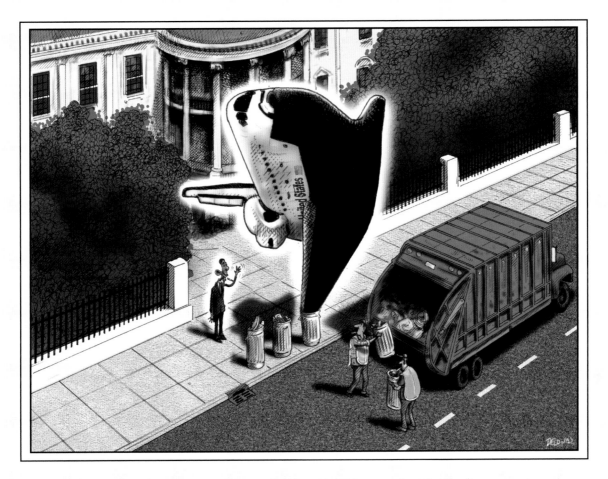

Obama cuts the space program and orders NASA to work with Muslim countries.

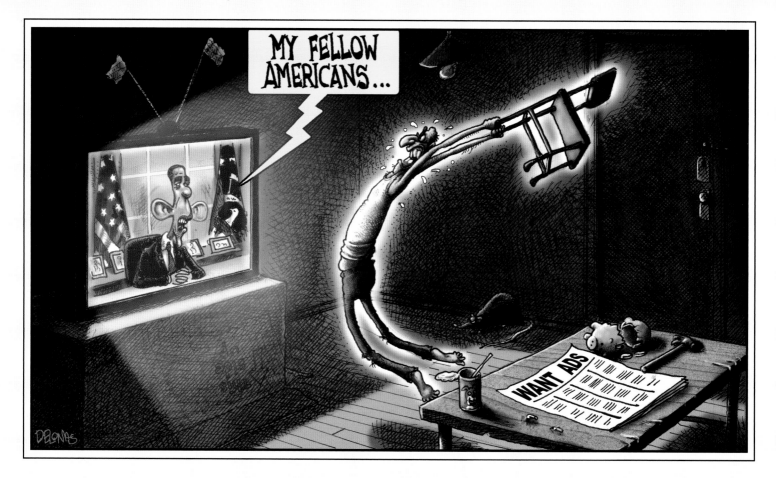

Obama addresses the country over the economic crisis.

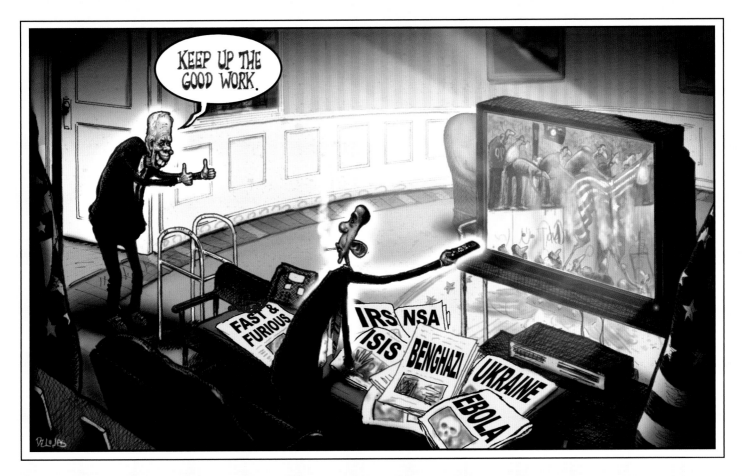

Carter no longer considered by many as the worst president.

SPORTS

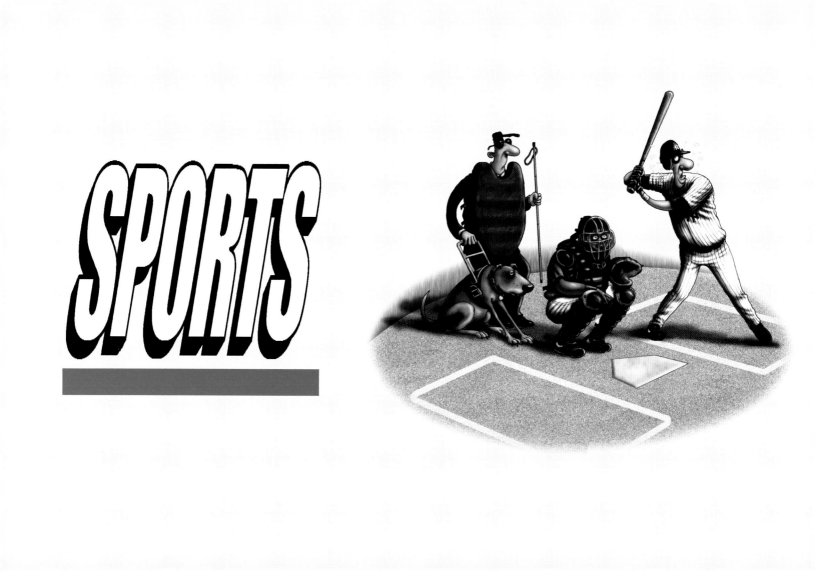

Foot Locker
REAL REFS ARE BACK... WE NEED OUR OLD JOBS BACK.

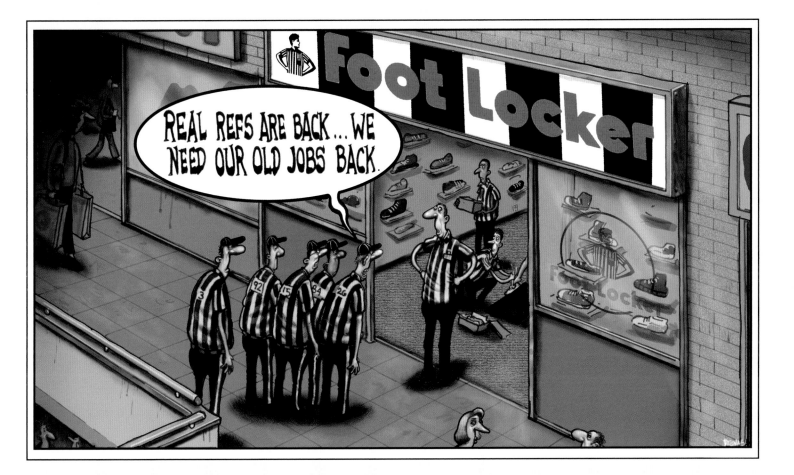

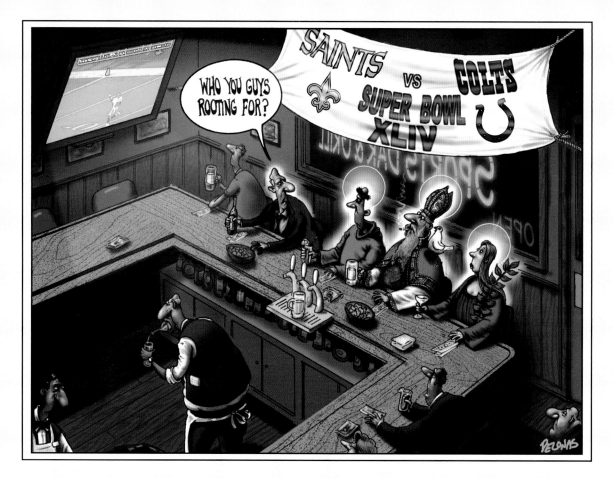

Super Bowl XLIV: Saints v. Colts.

BRETT FAVRE RESIGNS
THEY TOOK THAT WELL.
JETS

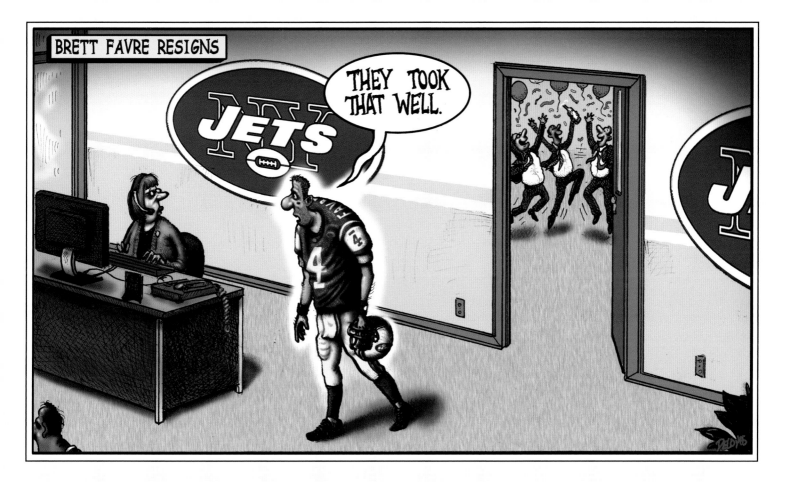

OKAY, OKAY, WE'LL WATCH SOMETHING ELSE!!!
VICK
7
EAGLES
DELWAS

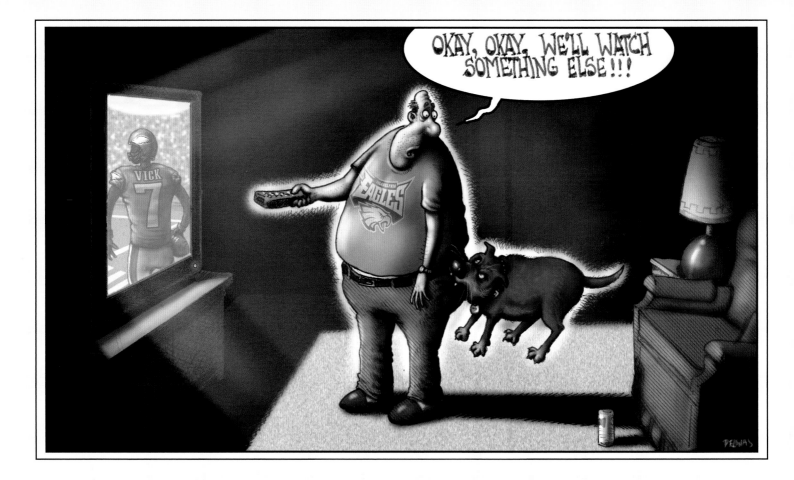

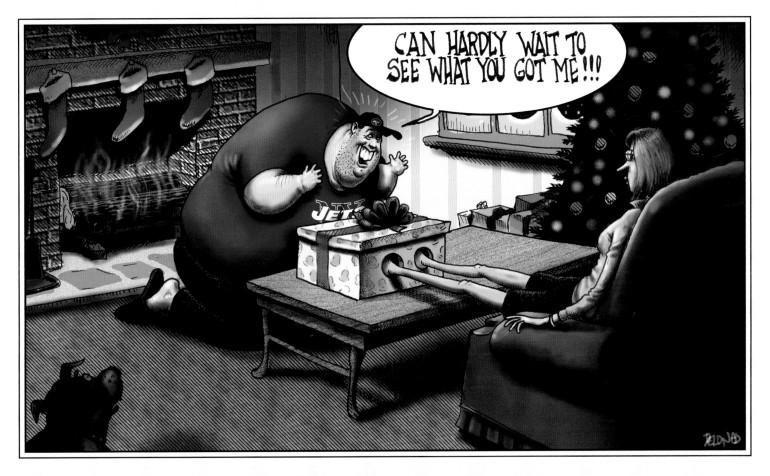

NY Jets head coach, Rex Ryan, has a foot fetish.

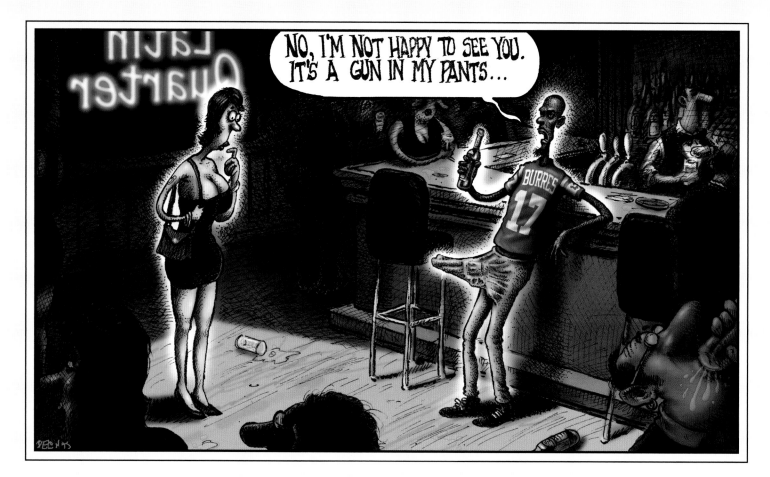

NY Giants receiver Plaxico Burress suffered an accidental gunshot wound from a gun hidden in his pants.

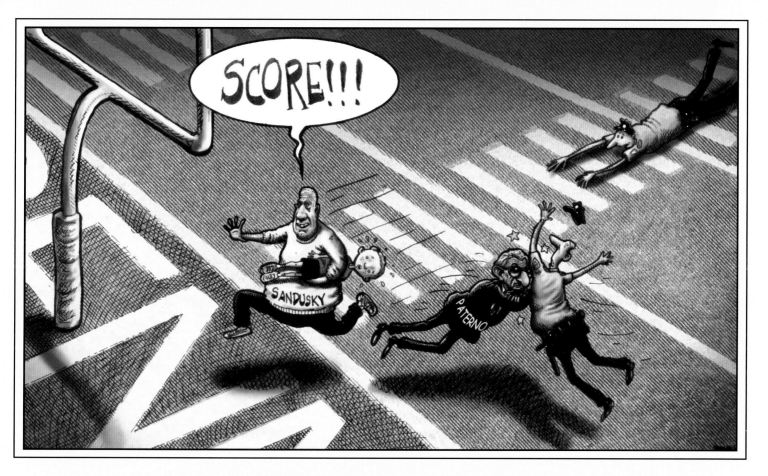

How assistant coach Jerry Sandusky was able to get away with molesting children for so long.

STOP PRESSING THE MUTE BUTTON AT ME!!!

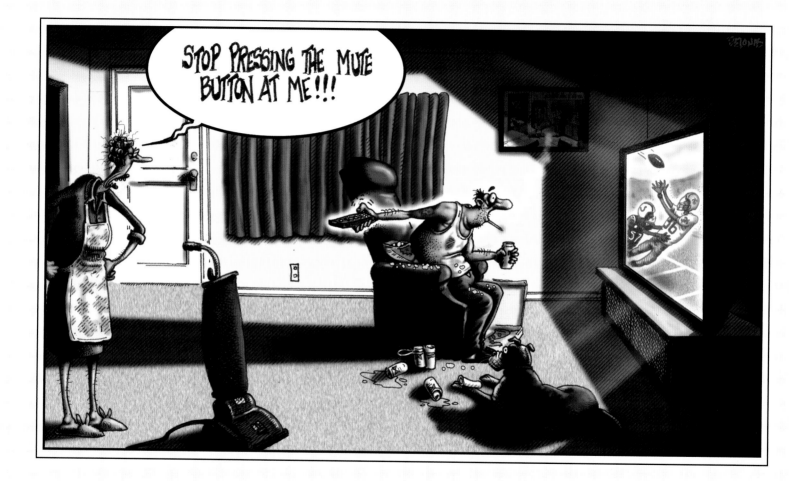

YOU'RE WATCHING THE SUPER BOWL, YOUR WIFE STARTS TO VACUUM...THEN WHAT HAPPENS?

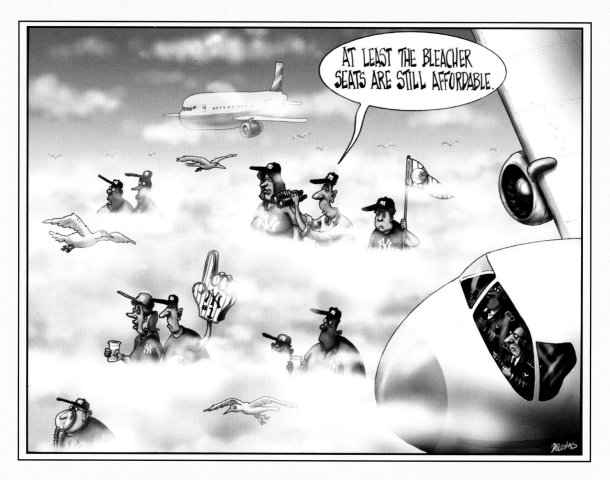

Yankee ticket prices soar but the bleacher seats are still affordable.

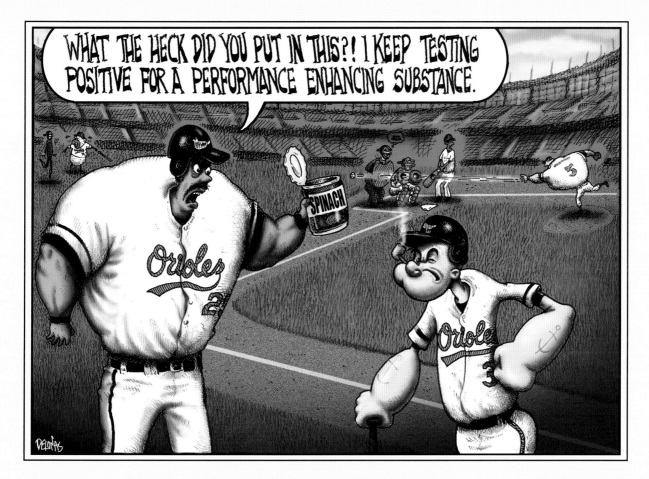

Baltimore Orioles's heavy hitter Raphael Palmeiro denies taking steroids despite repeatedly testing positive for them.

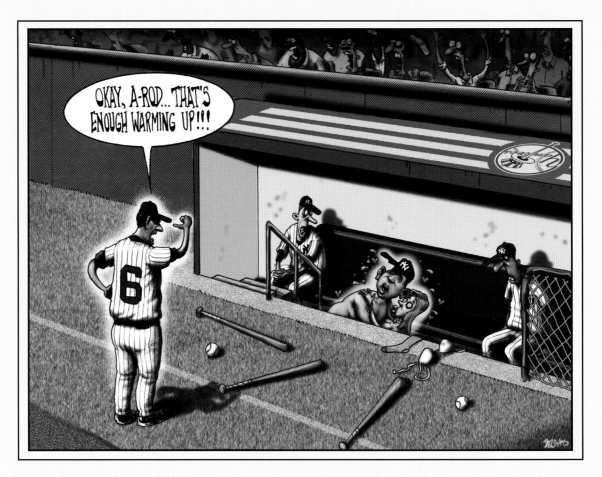

A-Rod has a lot of affairs.

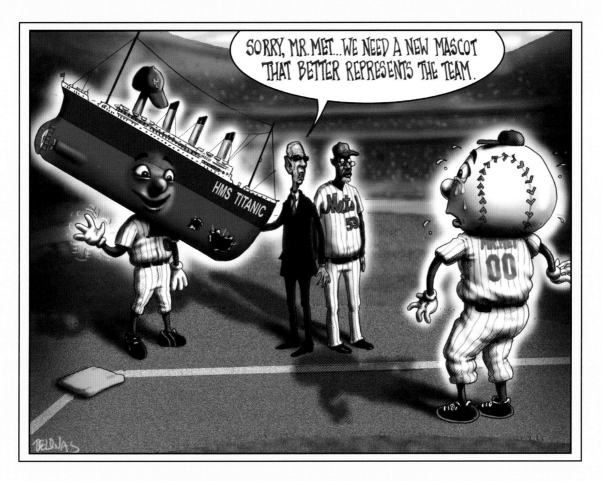

Should the Mets's mascot, Mr. Met, be replaced?

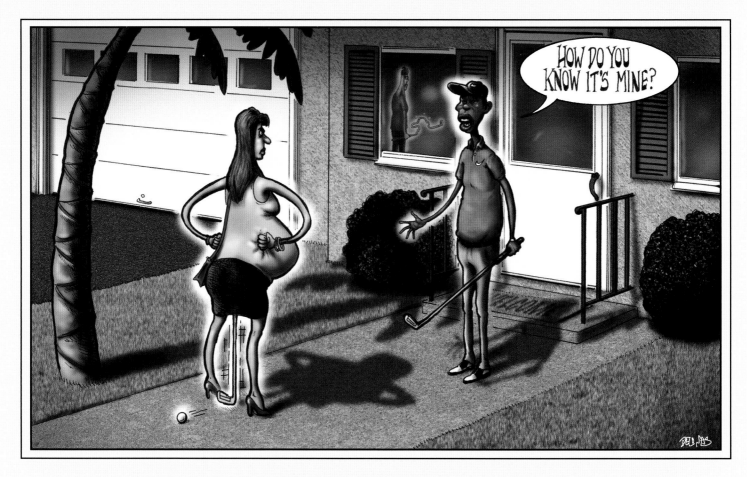

Tiger Woods's mistress is pregnant.

BRITISH SOCCER FANS
KICK IT, KICK IT, KICK IT...

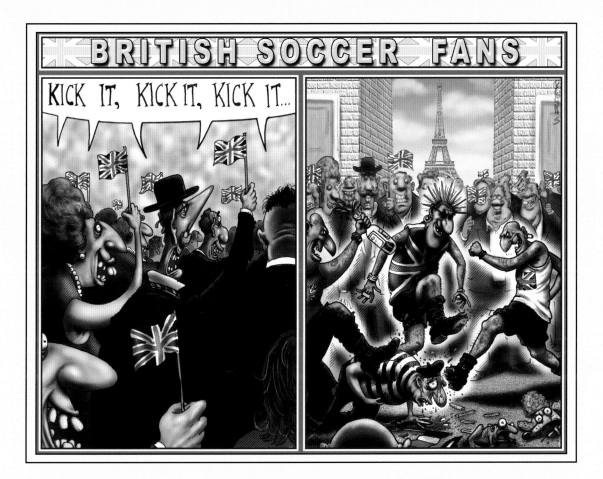

AND IN THIS CORNER...

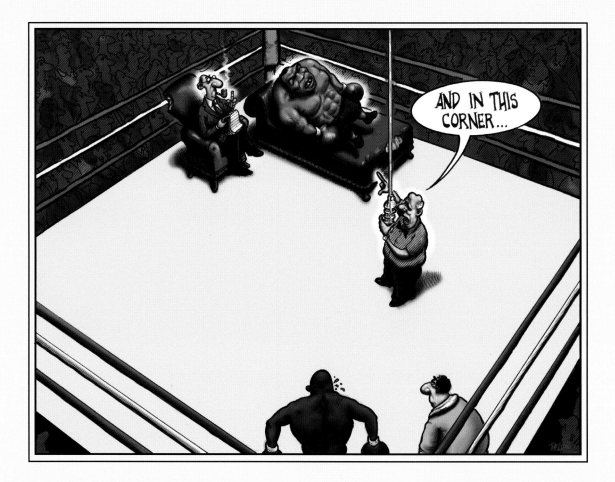

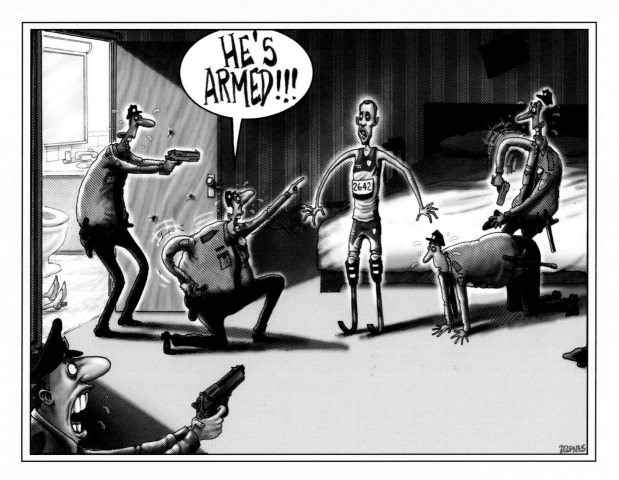

Legless African sprinter, Oscar Pistorius, shoots girlfriend.

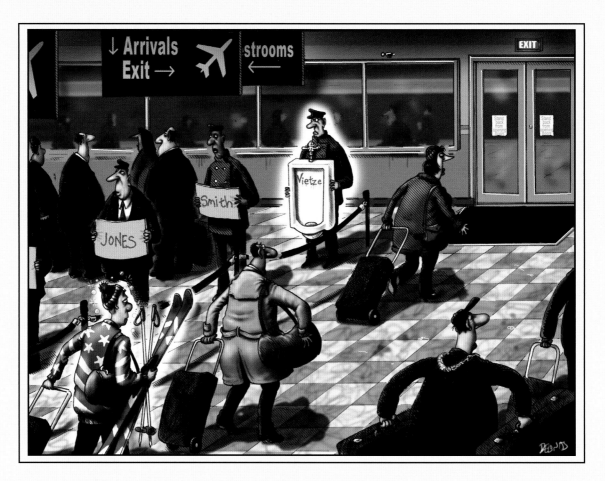

US skier Robert Vietze accused of peeing on twelve-year-old girl on a JetBlue flight.

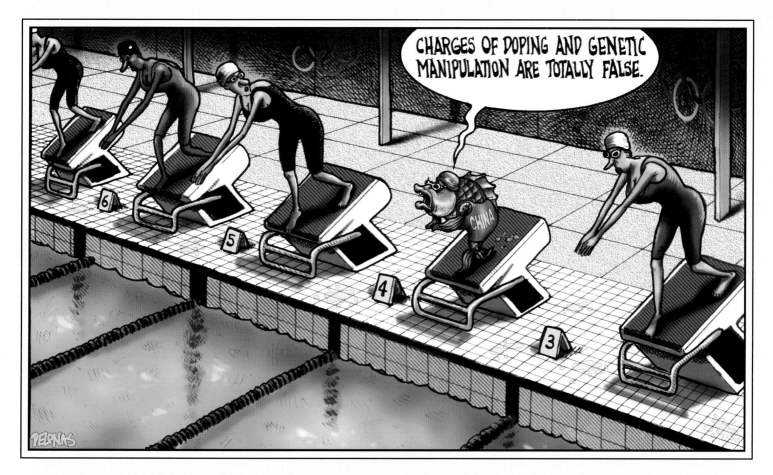

Accusations of doping and genetic manipulation at the 2008 summer Olympics in Beijing, China.

YOU'RE SPENDING TOO MUCH TIME WATCHING THE OLYMPICS.
0.1
DELONAS

WAR/TERRORISM

NEXT TIME, LET'S JUST DRIVE!!!
AIRPORT SEC

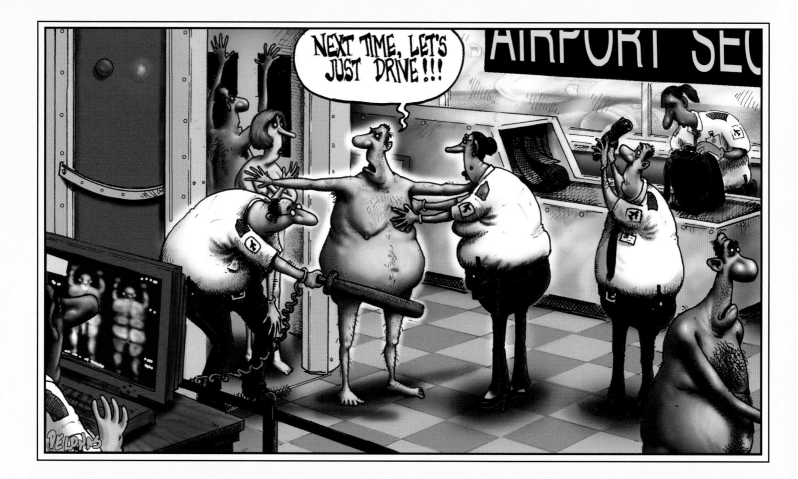

NEWARK
SORRY, YOU'RE ON THE NO-FLY LIST.
LINE STARTS HERE
DELONAS

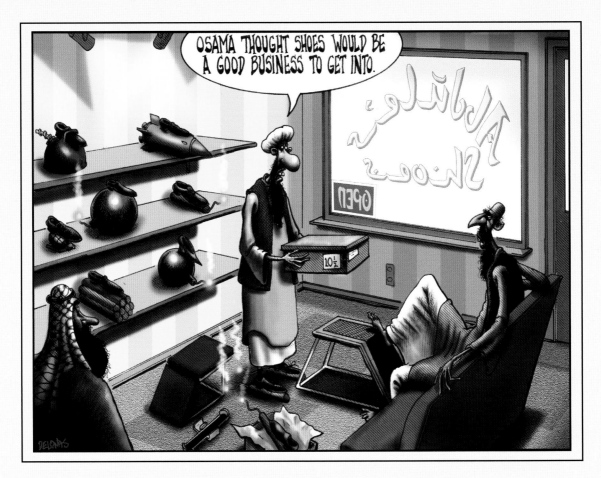

Terrorist Richard Reid tries to bring down Flight 63 with a shoe bomb.

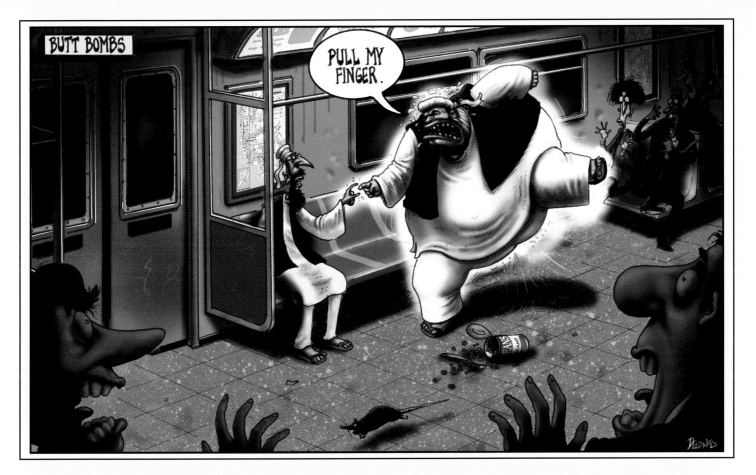

Butt bombs: Al Qaeda operatives found with explosives stuck up their rectums.

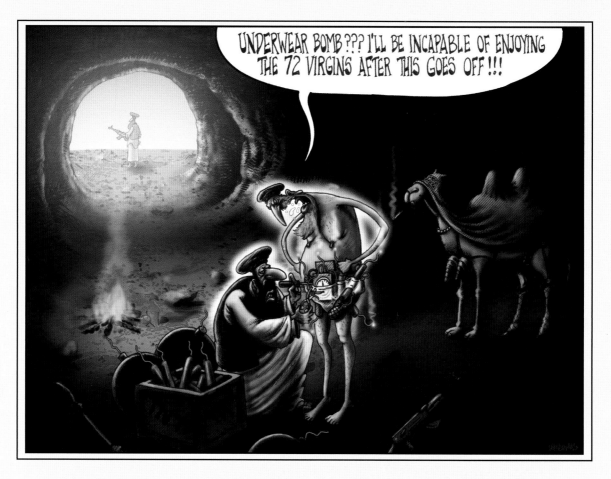

Underwear bomber Umar Farouk Abdulmutallab tries to bring down KLM Flight 588.

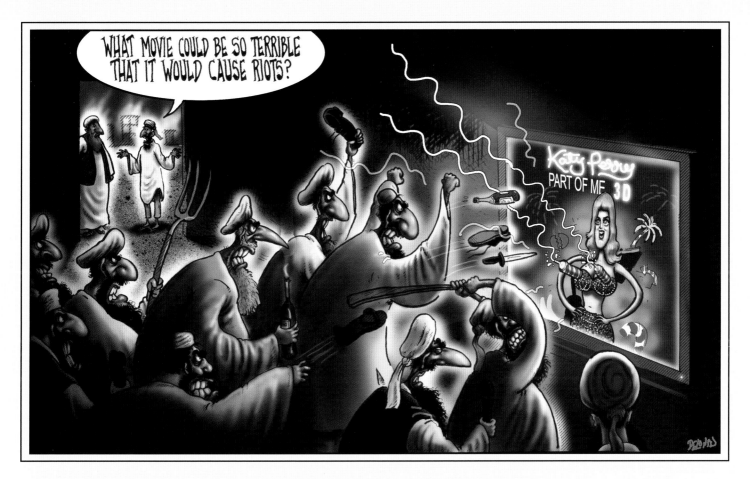

Benghazi attack blamed on film.

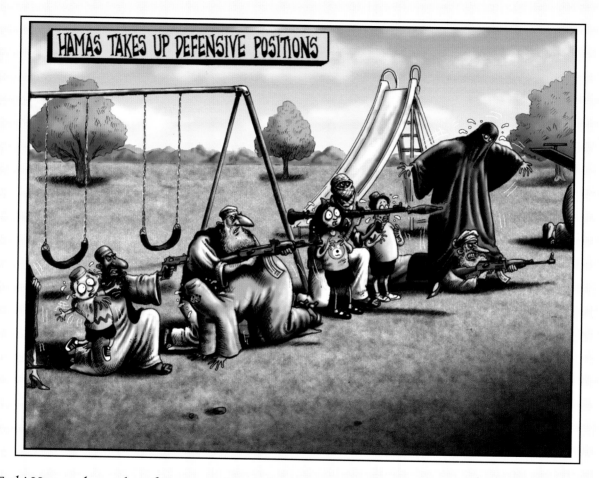

Fathi Hammad, member of Hamas and the Palestinian Council, said the groups deliberately use women and children as human shields.

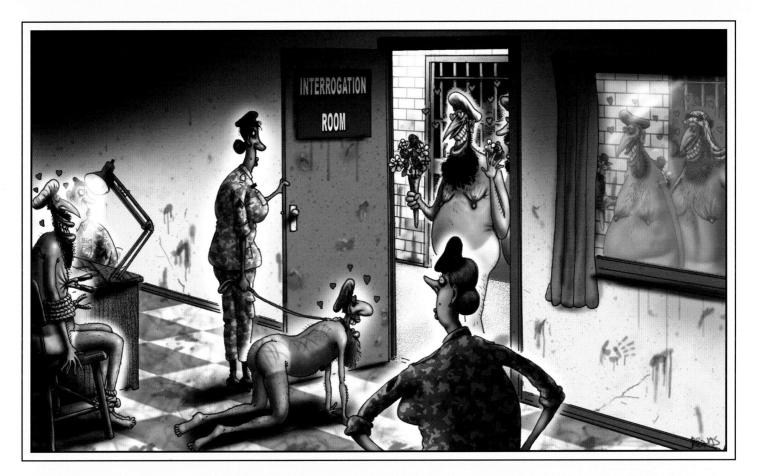

Photos surface of US soldier, Lyndie England, sexually abusing Muslim prisoners at Abu Ghraib.

LET ME GET THIS STRAIGHT...YOU'RE THE 72 VESTAL VIRGINS PROMISED TO ME FOR BEING A MARTYR???

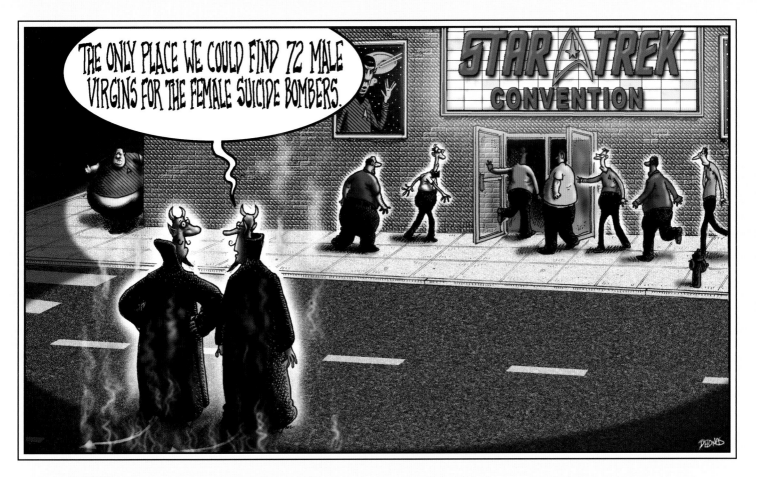

Al Qaeda starts using women suicide bombers. Do they receive the same reward as their male counterparts?

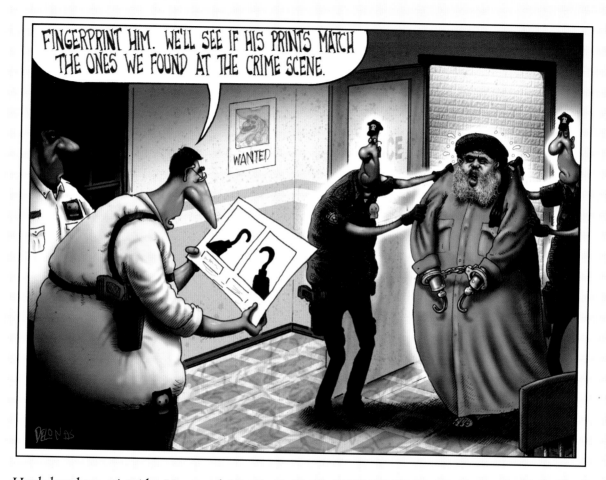

Hook-hand terrorist Abu Hamza al-Masri extradited to the United States for terror-related crimes.

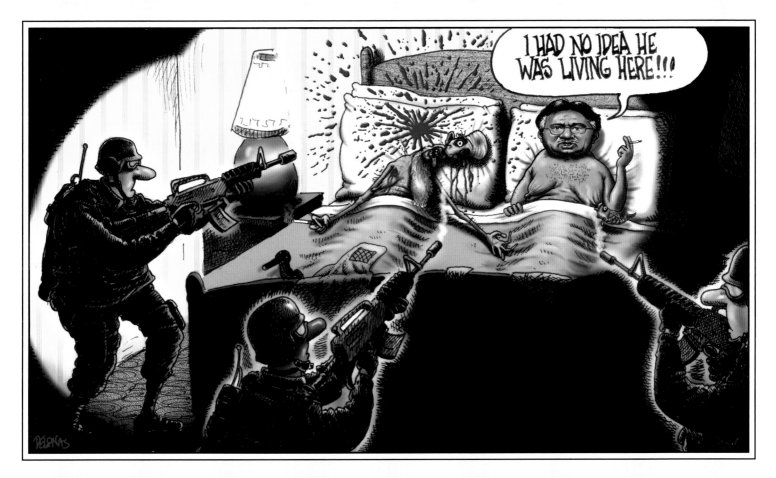

Osama Bin Laden was hiding in Pakistan.

THE PRESIDENT SAID TO BURY THE BODY AT SEA.

Burial at sea for Osama.

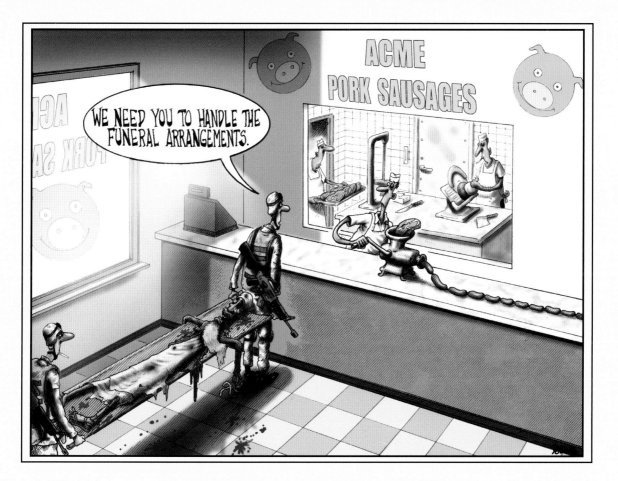

A better funeral arrangement for Osama Bin Laden.

DEFENSE CUTS
COVER ME!!!
DEDIAS

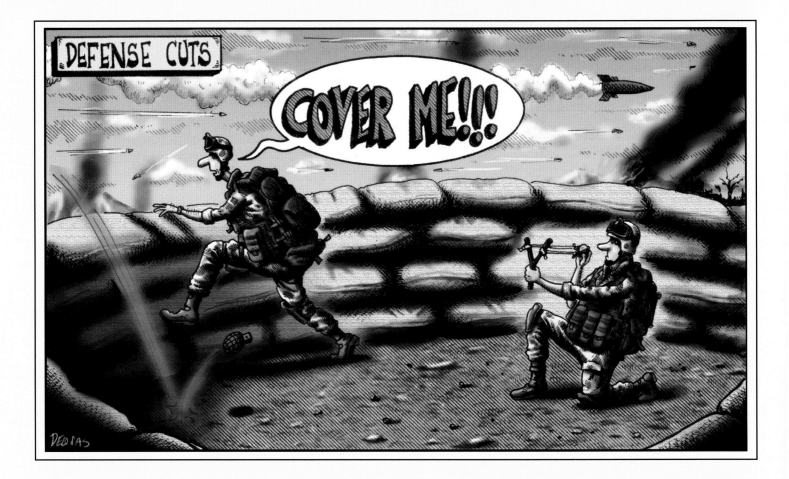

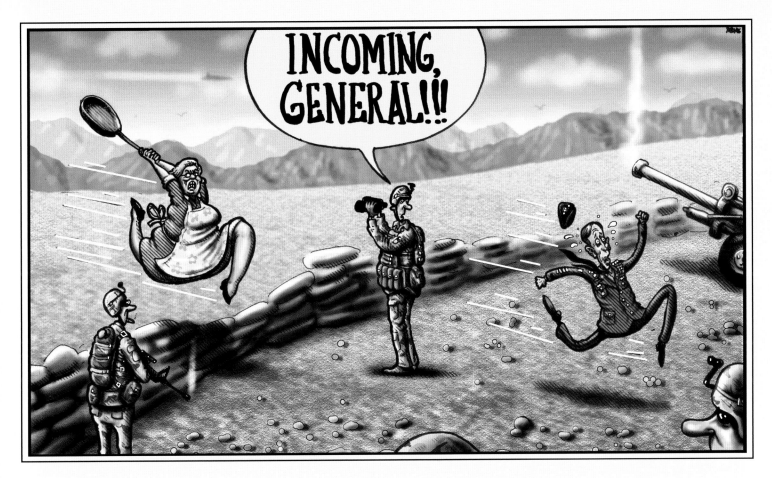

General Petraeus caught in an affair.

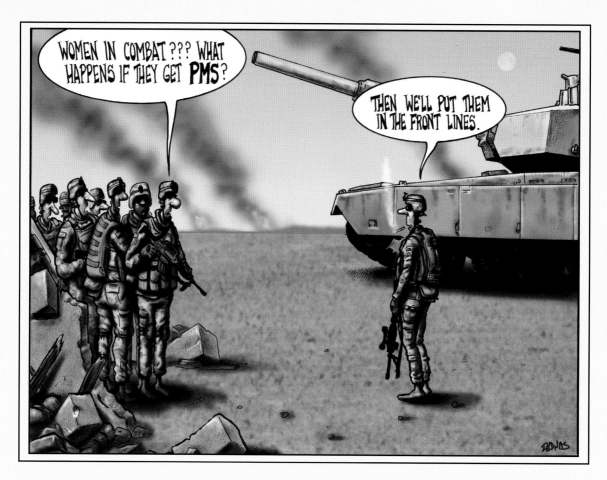

Military lifts ban on women in military roles.

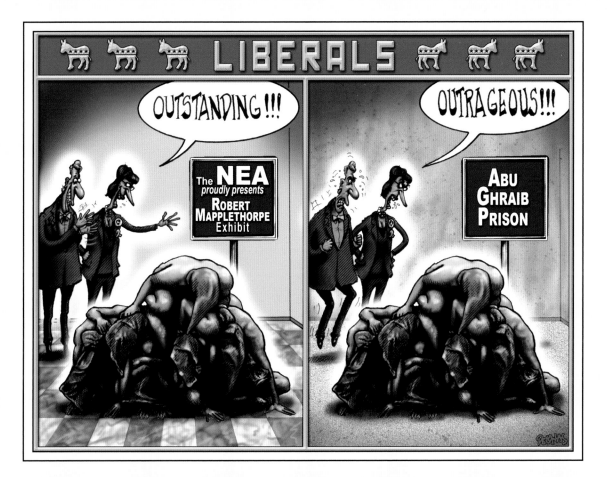

Liberals outraged by Abu Ghraib, Iraq.

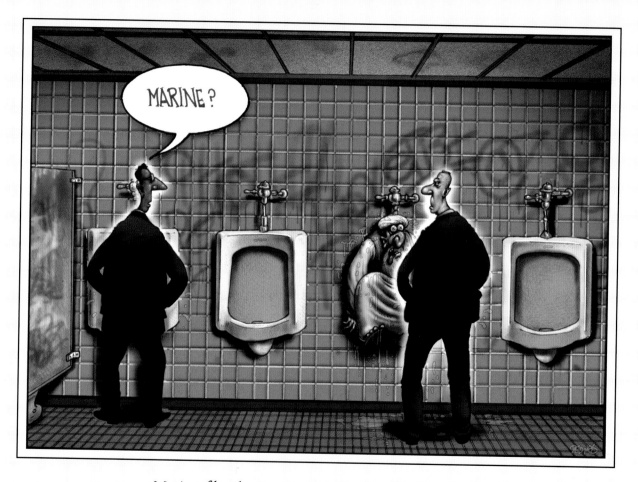

Marines filmed urinating on the bodies of dead Taliban.

WHAT'S THE PROBLEM WITH NORMALIZING RELATIONS WITH IRAN, BIBI?
DELONAS

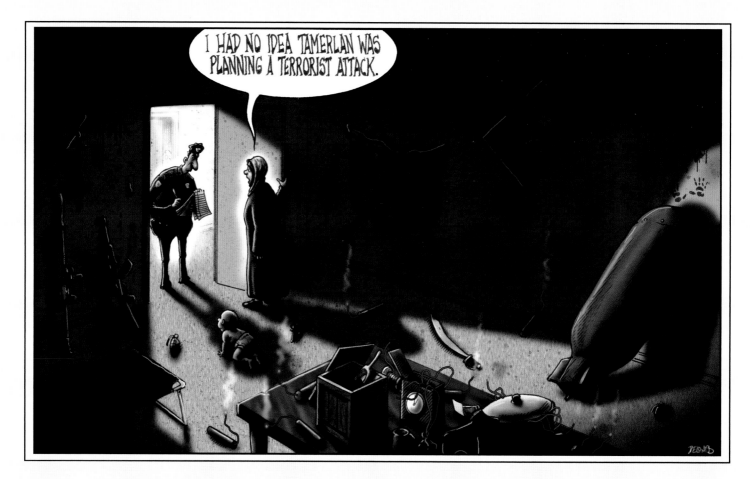

Boston Bomber Tamerlan Tsarnaev's wife was totally ignorant of his evil plot.

ALLAH AKBAR !!!

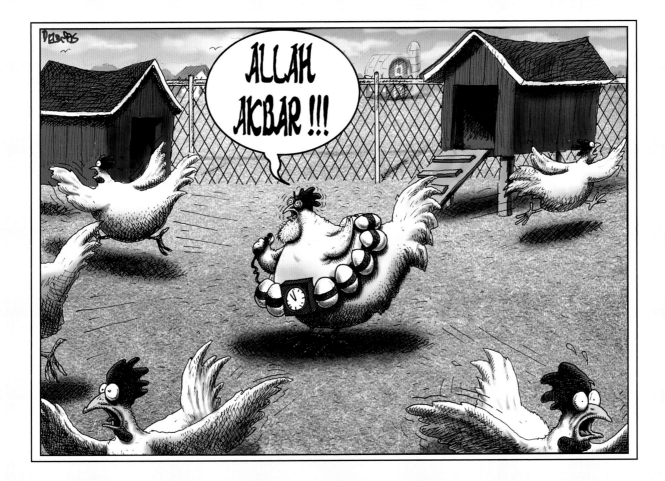

WORLD

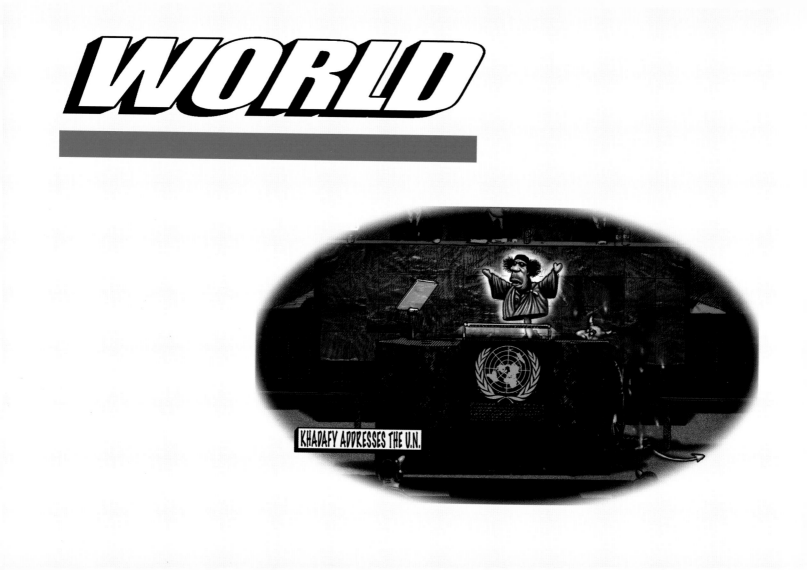

KHADAFY ADDRESSES THE U.N.

HOW CAN I STOP THE "HOT AIR" THAT'S MELTING THIS GLACIER?
HAVE YOU TRIED SHUTTING YOUR MOUTH?

Global warming.

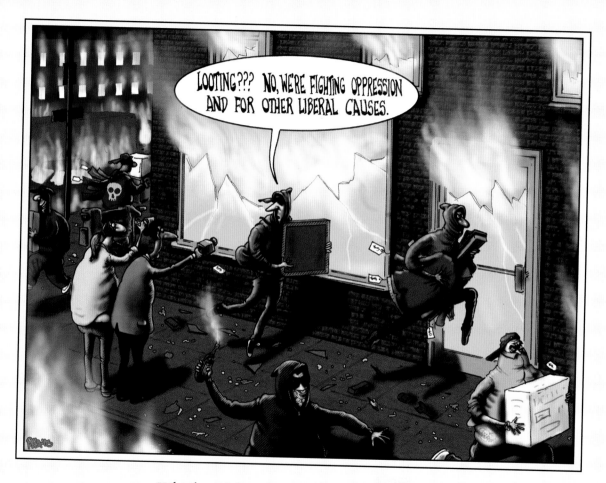

Why do socialist protests always involve looting?

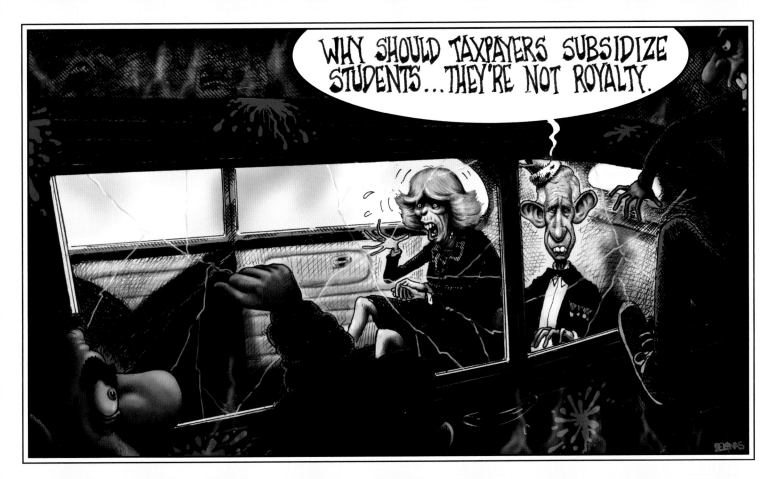

Prince Charles and Camilla Parker Bowles attacked by college students who are mad about their tuition subsidies being cut.

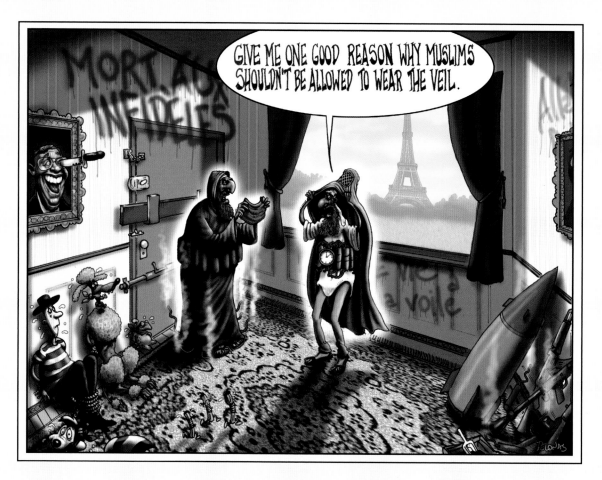

France tries to ban Muslim women from wearing the burka.

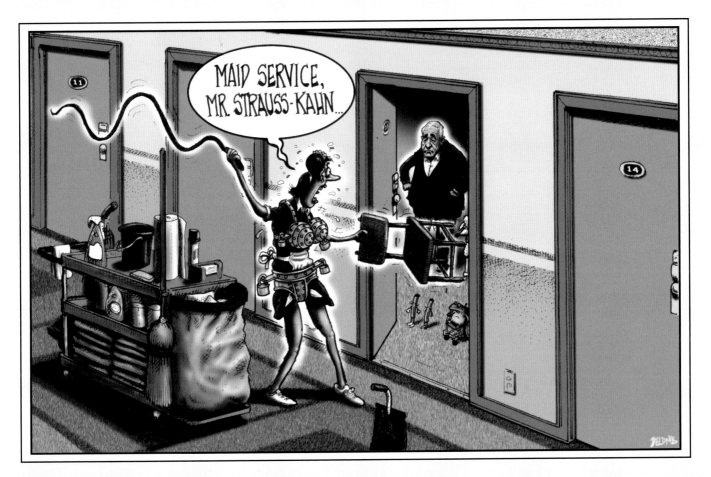

Former IMF chief, Dominique Strauss-Kahn, accused of raping a maid, Nafissatou Diallo, at the Sofitel Hotel, NYC.

DANG, I TOLD YUH TO PUT THE BUFFET IN THE MIDDLE OF THE SHIP!!!
CROWN PRINCESS
BUFFET
DELONAS

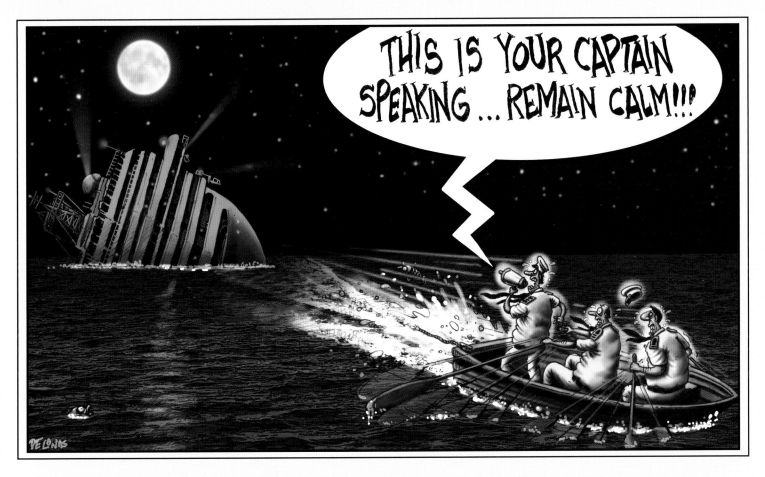

The Italian cruise ship, Costa Concordia, *partially sank as the captain abandons ship.*

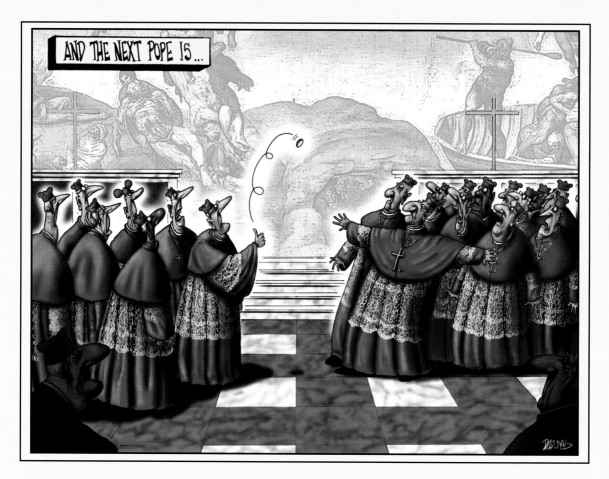

Conference of Cardinals meet behind closed doors to choose the next pope.

DEAD??? I DIDN'T EVEN KNOW KIM JONG WAS IL!!!
주체
DELONAS

Kim Jong-Il is dead.

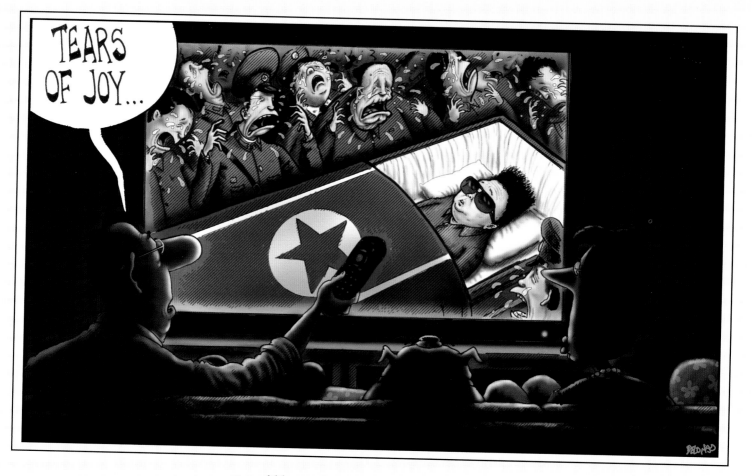

Incredible weeping at the death of Kim Jong-Il.

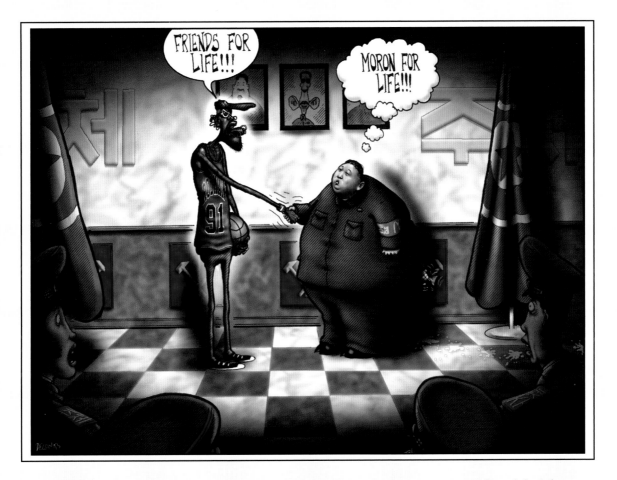

Dennis Rodman calls North Korea's murderous dictator Kim Jong-Un a "friend for life."

COVER HER !!! SHE NEEDS TO BE VEILED!!!
MUSLIM BROTHERHOOD

The Arab Spring.

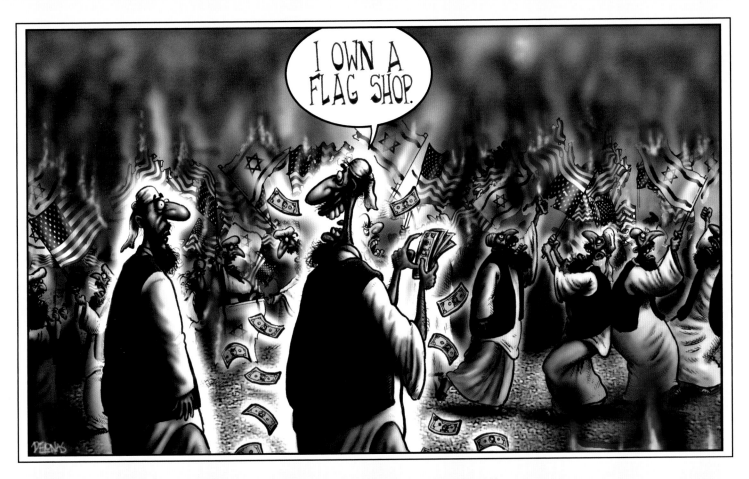

The business that I'd be in if I lived in the Middle East.

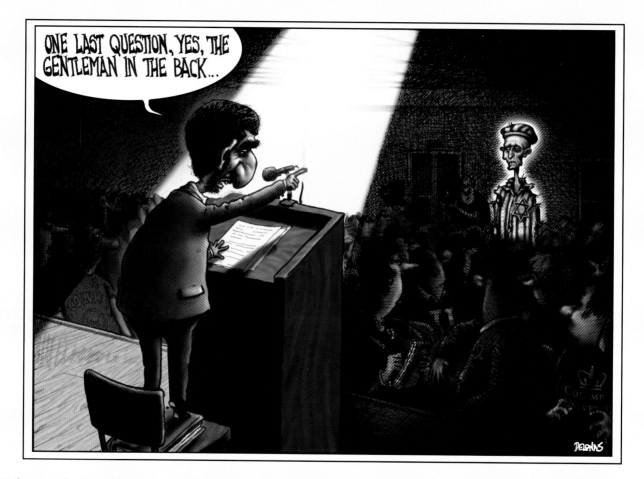

Holocaust denier and Iran's president Ahmadinejad has a question-and-answer session at Columbia University.

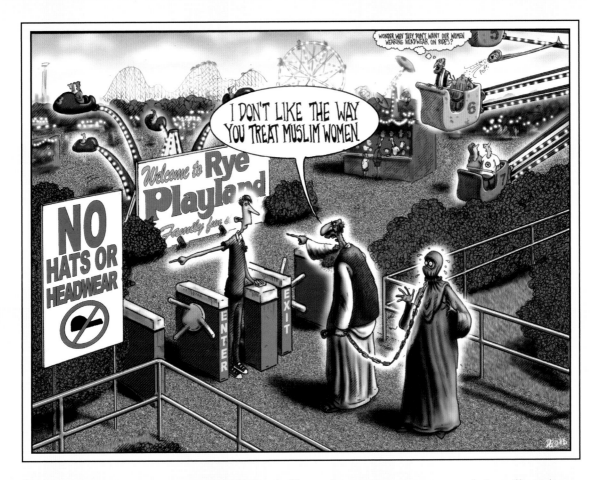

Muslims claim discrimination at Rye Playland, filing a lawsuit over women not being allowed to wear head scarves on certain rides.

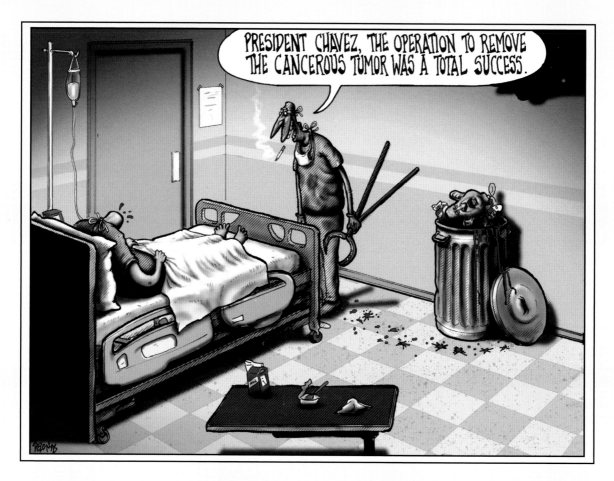

Hugo Chavez's cancer surgery.

LET'S PROTEST THE EVILS OF CAPITALISM ON FACEBOOK WITH OUR IPADS.
DOWN WITH CAPITALISM

ACKNOWLEDGMENTS

I would like to express my appreciation to the many people who contributed to my long career as a cartoonist at the *New York Post*. First, I must acknowledge the late, great cartoonist, Bay Rigby, who gave me a most coveted spot on Page 6; music critic Dan Aquilante, layout legend Frank LoMonte, and columnist Charlie Carillo for the countless times they helped me with cartoon ideas. Sincerest thanks to the many *New York Post* staff: my favorite Editor-In-Chief Ken Chandler, Carole Lee, Myron Rushetzky, Jim Pratt, Dennis Wickman, Linda Stasi, Lou Colasuonno, Xana Antunes, as well as owner Rupert Murdoch, and my great book agent Liza Fleissig.

Secondly, my thanks to the friendships and encouragement of Jim O'Connor, Michaela Scioscia, Dan Edwards, Al Hassinger, Nick Delonas, Cindy Casner, Michael Muntz, Ray O'Connor, Sam Farnon, Jim Reid, Jim Hoston, Will Wilson, Eric Goulder, and Chris Bilton.

Lastly, to Skyhorse Publishing for publishing this book and for their encouragement, guidance, and belief in this endeavor.